The U.S. Open

Game, Set, Unmatched

The U.S. Open

Game, Set, Unmatched

By Roger M. Williams

ACKNOWLEDGMENTS

The author and editors wish to acknowledge with grateful thanks the contributions of the following persons:

Harry Marmion, president; Ed Nussel, chairman, publications committee; Pierce O'Neil, director of sales and marketing; Page Crosland, director of communications; and Andre Christopher, senior writer, of the United States Tennis Association.

Sidney Wood, outstanding player of the Golden Age of tennis—and now a witty and wise senior statesman of the game—for sharing with the author his memories, impressions and analyses of the greats of his era and beyond.

Bud Collins, journalist, broadcaster and tennis historian—without equal—for writing (with Zander Hollander) *Bud Collins' Modern Encyclopedia of*

Tennis, from which the author drew liberally and with complete confidence in the accuracy of both facts and analysis.

Russ Adams, tennis photographer extraordinaire, and his staff for their assistance in providing us with so many of the pictures for this book.

The press departments of the Association of Tennis Professionals and the Women's Tennis Association— for quickly and cheerfully handling various requests.

The staffs of the International Tennis Hall of Fame and the Sports Illustrated Library for their invaluable research assistance.

Published by Time-Life Books

First printing
Printed in Hong Kong

Library of Congress Cataloging-in-Publication Data
The U.S. Open: Game, Set, Unmatched
          p.   cm.
   Includes index.
   ISBN 0-7835-5280-2
   1. U.S. Open Championships, New York,
   N.Y.—History. I.Time-Life Books.
   GV999.U12 1997
   796.342'09747'1—dc21

Vice President and Publisher: TERRY NEWELL
Associate Publisher: TERESA HARTNETT
Director of Editorial Development: JENNIFER PEARCE

CUSTOM PUBLISHING DIVISION
Vice President: MICHAEL HURLEY
Director of Strategic Partnerships: LAURIN ENSSLIN

TRADE DIVISION
Vice President of Sales: NEIL LEVIN
Director of Sales: LIZ ZIEHL

TIME-LIFE is a trademark of Time Warner Inc. USA

THE U.S. OPEN
was prepared by Bishop Books, Inc.
611 Broadway, New York, New York 10012
Project Director: MORIN BISHOP
   Senior Editor: CARRIE CHASE
   Copy Editor: JOHN BOLSTER
   Researcher: RACHAEL NEVINS
   Designer: BARBARA CHILENSKAS

CONTENTS

Introduction

No sport is an island; tennis, perhaps, least of all. The places that have accommodated the U.S. championships reflect the changing nature of the sport, the game, and the society that has shaped them.

The men's national tournament was first played (in 1881) in a venerable bastion of social privilege, the Casino at Newport, Rhode Island; the women's, (in 1887) in the only slightly lower-rung confines of the Philadelphia Cricket Club. After 3½ tranquil decades, the New York City borough of Queens muscled into the picture, and following a flurry of venue changes, the singles events settled into the West Side Tennis Club in the Queens village of Forest Hills.

There they both remained for 54 glorious years. The name Forest Hills came to connote top-quality tennis, although Wimbledon, calling itself rather smugly "The Championships," maintained an irreducible edge in prestige. The entire Golden Age of American tennis—the age of Bill Tilden, Don Budge, Helen Wills, Alice Marble, Jack Kramer, Pancho Gonzales—unfolded on the abused but hardy grass at "the West Side." So, too, on grass and then Har-Tru (a soft surface comparable to clay), did the just-as-golden age that followed, featuring Rod Laver and Ken Rosewall, Althea Gibson and Maureen Connolly, Margaret Smith Court and Billie Jean King, and budding superstars Jimmy Connors and Chris Evert. In the waning years of the venerable stadium but the springtime of their own lives, Jimmy and Chrissie captured each other's hearts as well those of millions of fans.

By the 1970s, society and tennis had changed even more drastically than during the sport's tenure at Newport, and the West Side stadium was plain out-of-date. The U.S. Tennis Association (USTA) decided to abandon Forest Hills for a Queens public park called Flushing Meadows. Since then, a new parade of heroes and heroines, too numerous to name here, has been marching across our court of dreams.

In the early 1990s, the USTA opted to finance a still-larger and more modern facility alongside the one it had been using in Flushing Meadows. In August 1997, the 117th renewal of the U.S. national championships unveiled a state-of-the-art sporting palace so new that some of the paint may still have been tacky. This facility memorialized not just growth or even tennis. The USTA named the creation, all $250 million-plus of it, for Arthur Ashe, the game's late, great player and statesman. One can hardly imagine a more fitting tribute or a more perfect union.

All that represents a long, very American journey, from a wooden and grassy enclosure reserved for the rich to a concrete and cement arena open to the world. The former inhabitants of the enclosure, looking down from their celestial sky box, must be amazed at the transformation.

• • •

At the Newport Casino, tennis historians tell us, the game was never really central. Socializing, with its attendant fripperies, held the stage. By 1881, when the first men's championship took place, the town's wealth and status had been raised to an all-time high by an influx of post–Civil War business barons. The big names among them remain familiar today: Vanderbilt, Astor, Belmont.

Snobbishness was intrinsic, but so was sport. Newport played host to yachting regattas and thoroughbred races, and, with their tennis franchise in hand, the local authorities would soon add other sporting innovations: the nation's first international polo match (in 1886) and first U.S. Open golf championship (in 1895).

Le tout-Newport turned out for the men's tennis tournament. If the tennis was a mere curiosity, the Casino and its crowd were true attractions. A contemporary travel writer described them: "There are probably few prettier scenes. . . . Perfectly trimmed lawns swept by the freshest and daintiest morning

The early days of U.S. tennis drew the cream of high society to the Newport Casino (right, in 1891) to watch "well-groomed young fellows ... obviously exhibiting both strength and skill."

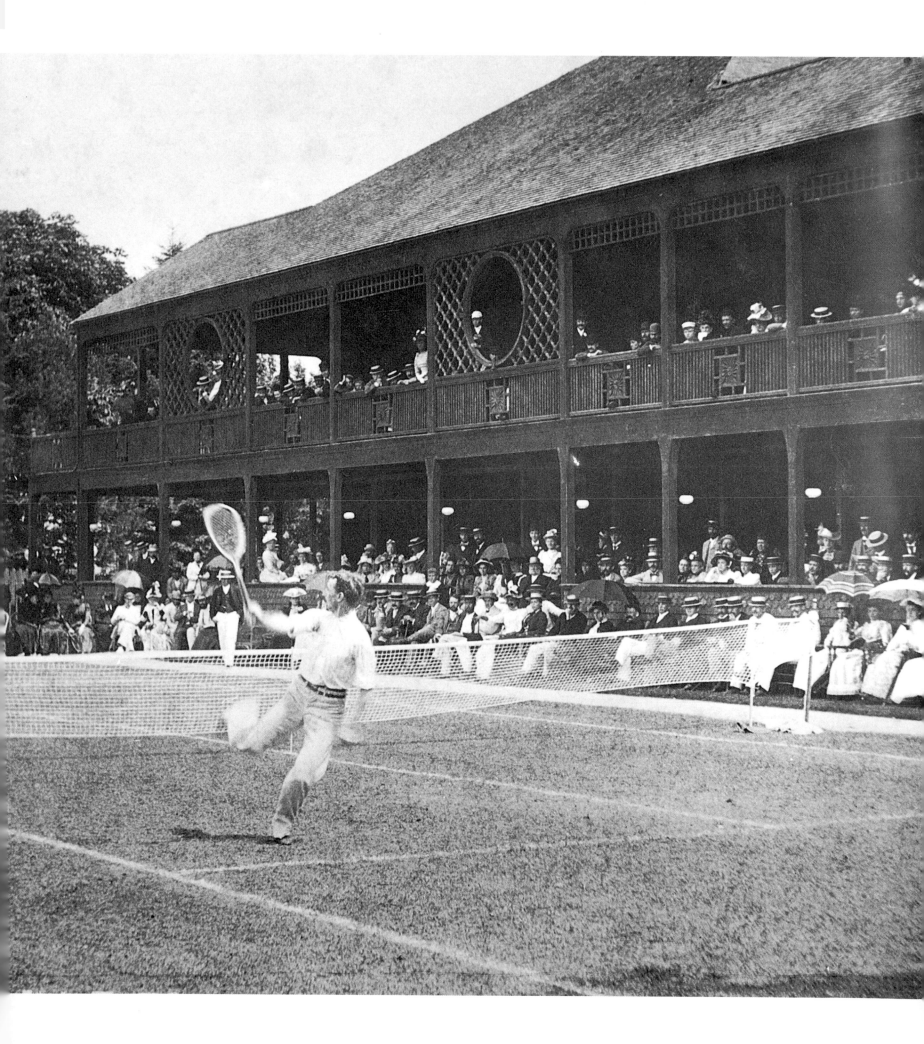

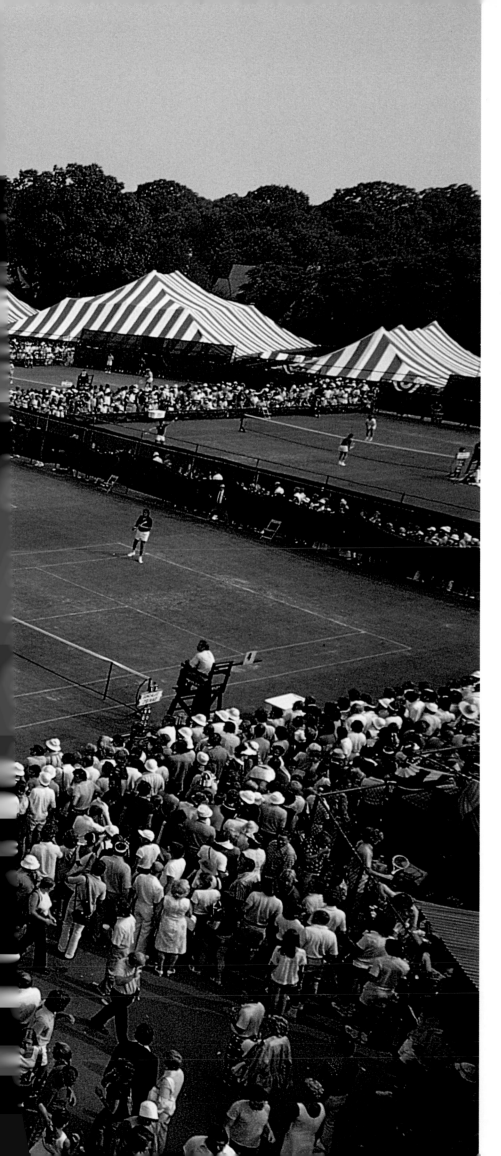

dresses, young men in flannels, rosy with health and irresponsibility ... and the well-groomed young fellows in the centre of the composition obviously exhibiting both strength and skill—make a picture which for combined animation and refinement, both of actors and spectators, it would be difficult to match anywhere."

Yet Newport was not secure as a tennis Mecca. Tennis then was largely a New York sport, and Newport's small spectator area, few and pricey hotels, traffic congestion, and social exclusiveness inevitably generated a rival bid from the Gotham to the south. In 1915, intense wrangling broke out among members of the then–U.S. National Lawn Tennis Association (USNLTA) over the prospect of moving to the West Side club. Traditionalist Newporters characterized the Queens venue as impossibly scruffy and predicted an unmanageable deluge of unqualified tournament entries if it landed the event. Nevertheless, the West Side prevailed in a close vote.

While the West Side club was building a stadium to augment its grandstand, the USLTA shipped the men's nationals down to Philadelphia in 1921, and sent the women's nationals in the reverse direction. In 1924 the two tournaments finally came to rest at the West Side.

By the 1970s, although its ivy-covered charm remained, the West Side stadium was creaking with age and inadequacy. In addition, as part of a private club in an egalitarian age, it projected a questionable image for the national championships. Some also considered it too small to "grow the game," as today's marketing executives would say, in the newly-arriving era of open tennis. Once the decision to move had been made, there was support for moving out of New York City altogether; the latter's oft-cited "deterioration" had weakened its hold on the championships.

The city found an unexpected and key supporter in a William E. "Slew" Hester, Jr. A Mississippian who believed in relocating within New York, Hester, as USTA president, chaired the committee that renovated an existing stadium in Flushing Meadows

Park in only 10 months and used it to anchor a complex called the USTA National Tennis Center. Thus the U.S Open migrated some 10 minutes in terms of auto travel but light years in terms of ambience and public-vs.-private philosophy.

Some traditionalists and other observers decried the change, and they raised loud objections to the Flushing Meadows site. "Cheap, carnival milieu" was a typical complaint, with critics citing everything from the steepness of the seating to the newly demonstrative crowds to the "shriek" of planes, outbound from LaGuardia Airport, that passed directly overhead. The new digs' defenders welcomed the more relaxed, socially leveling atmosphere. Both Connors and Ilie Nastase spoke warmly of Flushing. Said Nastase, "The crowd is very wild, very noisy. I love it." And Hester, the tennis center's master developer, pronounced the new location and its tournament "as American as apple pie."

They also were, and are, as New York as a bagel with a "schmear."

Flowers and greenery surround the center, but its core, like the city's, remains concrete and cement. Spectators cheer and sometimes jeer out loud— echoing the sounds from baseball's nearby Shea Stadium. Thousands arrive and depart on rumbling subway trains. The concessions serve food far more varied and cosmopolitan than can be found at stadiums elsewhere. Wimbledon (or Forest Hills) it ain't, but so what, already?

(Critics seldom credit the Flushing court surface, DecoTurf II, a medium-speed asphalt-based material that favors neither offense nor defense and therefore offers a fair test of competitive skills.)

When the USTA deemed its stadium no longer adequate, the issue of staying in New York again arose. Airplane fly-overs were aggravating everybody, and the issue of a new facility became entangled in big-city politics. At least two other cities received serious consideration. "We wouldn't have built the new Flushing stadium without an agreement not to fly over it during the Open," says David Markin, the former USTA president who chaired the building committee. "It took two years to work that out with city and borough officials and the Federal Aviation Administration."

The political considerations centered on the use of additional parkland and the jockeying between mayoral candidates David Dinkins and Rudolph Giuliani. Incumbent Mayor Dinkins, a rabid tennis fan and big supporter of a new stadium, signed the enabling legislation at the very end of his term, leaving Giuliani, his successor, powerless to reverse it.

So a majestically imposing, technologically advanced, 23,000-seat stadium arose on the expanded USTA site. It makes up all the shortcomings of its predecessor (which is being renovated and downsized for continued use) and then some. Meanwhile, the entire center has been expanded, with the total number of courts increasing from 39 to 47. As in the past, the entire place is open to the tennis-playing public 300 days a year. And what a place from the standpoint of John Q. Tennis.

Memories of Opens past grace each court, and as Jana Hunsaker of the center staff notes, "Nowhere else can you play where the courts are resurfaced every year."

There was strong sentiment on the USTA board to put the organization's name on the new stadium. Happily, that idea was overtaken by a much better one: to name the facility for the person who, across the history of tennis, best combined ability, gentle-manliness, thoughtfulness, and personal commitment to high values.

The USTA took the occasion to hold a press conference in New York City. President Harry Marmion choked up as he announced the decision to call the facility "Arthur Ashe Stadium." Clearly, he was happy that the USTA board had taken the principled, rather than the commercial, road in naming the facility. When Marmion cued up a video of Ashe highlights, the sense of loss—for

tennis, for America, for humanity—was palpable.

Jeanne Moutoussamy-Ashe, Arthur's wife, spoke affirmatively of her husband's commitment to the USTA and to New York. "We are enormously proud of you, Arthur," she said. Then Mayor Giuliani stepped to the microphone, and a slight tension could be felt throughout the room. What would Giuliani, at times a bitter critic of the new stadium deal, have to say? Only nice things, it turned out. He praised Ashe in a sophisticated manner: "an absolutely transforming figure . . . an example of the way to behave when we are under pressure and in very difficult circumstances." He even managed to declare of the USTA and its new stadium, "the City of New York is grateful that you are doing this."

So now, and for many, many years to come, it's "Linesmen ready? Play," in the Arthur Ashe Stadium at the USTA National Tennis Center.

Simply the Place to Be

As the last hints of summer fade from the September air, the U.S. Open has always been the place to be for New Yorkers and for tennis fans of every stripe. Even in the more genteel Forest Hills days, the legendary Tudor clubhouse (left) drew tennis-hungry hordes who packed the stands (right), sometimes forcing unfortunates without a seat to take unusual measures (below) to sneak a peek at the action.

When the tournament moved to Flushing in 1978, the crowds followed and in far greater numbers as the tournament took on an even more distinctly New York flavor, complete with food courts (above), which served up a dizzying array of cuisines, and a spanking new stadium (top) that could accommodate the huge, vocal and highly partisan crowds which streamed up its walkways (right).

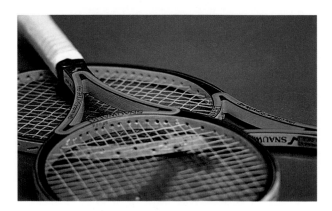

And what are all the fans and officials scrutinizing with such intensity? The players, of course, whose life under the microscope has produced a variety of responses, including the collected calm of Billie Jean King in 1967 (below); the smiles of then-couple Chris Evert and Jimmy Connors (far right, above) in 1974; the exultation of Steffi Graf in 1995 (far right); and—who could forget?—a volcanic tantrum from John McEnroe in 1981 (right).

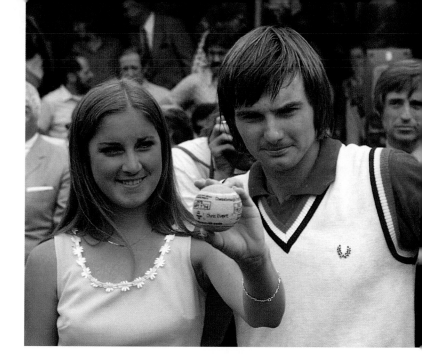

Celebrity Corner: The Open always attracts its share of glitterati from the worlds of entertainment and high society, including (clockwise from right): Bill Cosby in 1986; Johnny Carson in 1987; Yoko Ono and Sean Lennon in 1986; Brooke Shields in 1995; then vice-presidential candidate Geraldine Ferraro in 1984; Kirk Douglas in 1985; the former Duchess of York in 1996; and the New Yorker's New Yorker, Alan King, in 1978.

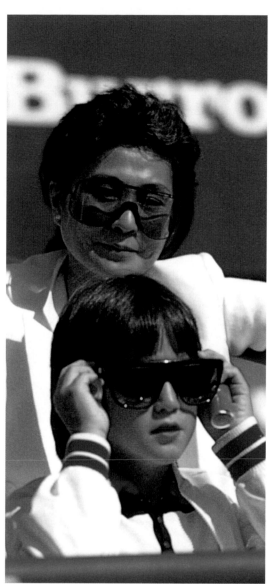

While the weather often cooperates, producing a sun-dappled day for an old-timer examining the champions of yore (far left, above), a well-warmed back for a crew member preparing to raise the net (far left, below) and a sensational sunset for all to enjoy (below), sometimes the fates are less kind as rains force the squeegee crew into action (left) and tax the capacity of a still-cheerful couple's umbrella (above).

FIRST SET:

THE PRE-OPEN ERA 1881–1967

FIRST SET
The Pre-Open Era
1881–1967

In 1881, when Richard Sears took the court against William E. Glyn at the Newport Casino in the first U.S. national singles championship, the event was a transatlantic hybrid. U.S. officials adopted the rules of Wimbledon, which England had inaugurated four years earlier; Glyn and some others among the 25 competitors were British; and the players swatted a British ball made of rubber covered in felt. On the other hand, the event was overseen by the U.S. National Lawn Tennis Association—the world's first national tennis governing body; the nets stood one foot lower than Wimbledon's; and the winner was a

Harvard student, Sears, who beat his British opponent easily. Sears went on to capture the national title in each of the next six years, retiring (presumably due to boredom) at the age of 25. Sears liked Newport's lower, sloping net because, he later wrote, "I had taken up a mild form of volleying [then a great novelty] . . . and all I had to do was to tap the balls as they came over . . . running my opponent all over the court." Under the "challenge" system, Sears and several successors as champions had to play only the survivor of an "all-comers" event. (The system lasted until 1912 for men and

Key figures from the early years of the tournament include: the Big Four (above, from left, Bertha Townsend, Margarette Ballard, *Louise Allderdice and Ellen Hansell); powerful Molla Mallory (above, right), who won eight singles title between 1915 and '26;* *and Richard Sears (far right), winner of the first seven men's singles titles, and U.S. tennis pioneer James Dwight.*

Two of the game's most popular stars meet in the 1936 final as Fred Perry (in hat) defeats Don Budge in a marathon seesaw battle, 2–6, 6–2, 8–6, 1–6, 10–8. It is the third and final singles title for Perry.

1919 for women before giving way to the democratic method of tossing the champ in with the rabble.)

The most important competitor at Newport in 1881 played only doubles. He was Dr. James Dwight. He had already been so active in the sport and so instrumental in the development of the U.S. Championships that some have called him the father of American tennis. Dwight's partner was Sears, and not quite coincidentally, they were cousins. Tennis was an upper-crust, Eastern family/college affair in those days. Dwight and Sears were neighbors on Boston's Beacon Street; Sears's grandfather was the city's wealthiest resident.

The women's national singles began six years later in Philadelphia. Three of the so-called Big Four competitors, all from the city's Belmont Cricket Club, entered the draw, and one of them, Ellen "Nellie" Hansell, took the title. They all hit sidearm serves and sliced ground strokes, and never, ever came to net. In their long-sleeved shirts and dresses, dashing about in the summer heat, they must have suffered mightily.

Shaping the entire 87-year era was a peculiar financial system. Tennis had begun as a purely amateur sport; and although professional play eventually took hold, the amateur ideal and practice retained a remarkably tenacious hold on the U.S. championships and all other major events. Players officially received only expenses; the best of them also received under-the-table payments that led to widespread cynicism and charges of "shamateurism."

Yet from the standpoint of quality of play, the game at the top level suffered little, even though promoters began regularly picking off the No. 1 amateurs to add to the ongoing pro tour. Great players continued to develop and thrive under the supposedly amateur system. A few even managed to thrive under it financially: Bill Tilden spent freely, and Bobby Riggs was on the personal payroll of a Wall Street mogul; in 1939, Riggs also won more than $100,000—a fortune in those days—betting on himself to win Wimbledon.

The fact that any really good player could make a nice living playing tennis on the tour lured more and more sons and daughters of the working class, most of whom had honed their skills in public

CLASSIC MATCHES

1926 QUARTERFINAL: BILL TILDEN VERSUS HENRI COCHET

France's Four Musketeers had arrived. They could be difficult, and Cochet was the best of them. But Tilden was Tilden: champion at Forest Hills in each of the previous six years, the "Mt. Everest of tennis." Tilden was, however, eight years Cochet's senior, and he had hurt his knee a week earlier. Cochet bothered him even more than the knee. Absorbing the speed of the American's serves and ground strokes, and varying the pace and placement of his own shots, Cochet outmaneuvered the great tennis thinker. Cochet also volleyed magnificently, charging the net repeatedly despite his opponent's mastery of the passing shot. In order to reduce the strain on his injured knee that chasing balls in the backcourt would impose, Tilden relied to an unusual degree on his net game. So intense was the interest in the match that tournament officials absentmindedly neglected to start the other quarterfinals until this contest ended. After winning an extended first set, Tilden lost the next two quickly. At that point, *The New York Times*'s Allison Danzig wrote, "He won the hearts of the 9,000 spectators . . . as he had never won them in victory." Trailing 1–4 in the fifth set, Tilden evened it at 4–all with sensational net play. He proceeded to take a 6–5 lead but then crumbled before Cochet's "counter-strokes of craft," winning only four points in the last three games. For the Musketeers, the victory marked the opening assault of their three-year conquest of the citadel of American tennis.

1949 FINAL: PANCHO GONZALES VERSUS TED SCHROEDER

Although Gonzales was the defending title holder, most experts expected Schroeder to beat him. Gonzales had been dubbed a "cheese champion" because of losses to inferior players earlier in the year, while Schroeder had just won Wimbledon and was expected to be the next amateur chosen to join the pro tour. Besides, Schroeder had beaten Gonzales in seven of their eight previous meetings and had gained fame for his ability to pull out long matches. The first set of this one equaled many three-setters in length. It went 18–16 to Schroeder, with "Gorgo"—for gorgonzola, as in cheese champion—suffering a bad line call on a critical point in the 33rd game. When Schroeder ran through the second set, 6–2, the match was as good as over. But Gonzales roared back to take the third with the loss of only 14 points and the fourth by an easy 6–2. In the fifth, Gonzales broke serve at 4–all. The tenth game was ragged, with only one winning shot. Schroeder overhit one last forehand and stood stunned: game, set, match—Gorgo.

parks. That social change overlapped a regional change in which the rest of the country, especially California, caught up with the East in producing tennis champions. Maurice McLoughlin pioneered in that respect. Son of an Irish immigrant and product of the parks, nicknamed "Red" (for his hair, not his politics), McLoughlin won the national singles in 1912 and '13.

In the 1930s, and right through the '40s and '50s, a trickle of top Californians became a deluge. The domineering but dedicated president of the Southern California Tennis Association, Perry T. Jones, nurtured most of them: Riggs, Ellsworth Vines, Gene Mako, Jack Kramer, Maureen Connolly, Louise Brough, Pancho Gonzales, and many more. Still others—Don Budge, Alice Marble, et al.—came from the northern part of the state. (Even so, the Ivy League raised its head on one stunning occasion. In 1930, playing California's John Doeg, ranked No. 1 in the country, W. Barry Wood, a football All-America and Phi Beta Kappa at Harvard, pushed the match to the full five sets before losing.) The rest of the country was represented by such players as Milwaukee's Frank Parker; Gardnar Mulloy, out of Miami; Globe, Arizona's Helen Jacobs; and, from Atlanta, Bryan "Bitsy" Grant (at 5' 4", 120 pounds, the best really small male player in history). All except Grant would win multiple titles at Forest Hills.

Much earlier, and from much farther away, came "Molla" Bjurstedt Mallory. After learning the game during Norway's fleeting summers, Mallory hit World War I–era U.S. tennis like a hurricane, winning the U.S. singles title a record eight times. Built more like a male fullback than a female tennis player, she had only one big shot, a crunching forehand. But with it she bludgeoned even the legendary (and melodramatic) Suzanne Lenglen when, in 1921, *la Lenglen* made her only foray to the U.S. Nationals.

After Mallory, and except for the lone British champion, Fred Perry, foreigners hit Forest Hills in packs and periodic waves.

France's debonair Four Musketeers—Rene Lacoste, Henri Cochet, Jean Borotra, Jacques Brugnon—pried loose the United States's grip on its

tournament in the late 1920s, and regiments of Harry Hopman–trained Australians periodically pulverized it in the 1950s and '60s. Women from overseas had no corresponding success. Between Mallory and Aussie Margaret Smith in 1962—a stretch of 36 years—foreigners won only three times.

In the eyes of some, there were two Forest Hills champions who, though from the U.S., were considered greater interlopers than the foreign titlists. Althea Gibson and Arthur Ashe, both of whom were black, each won the singles title within 10 years of one another. Gibson had to struggle merely to gain a place in the draw. When she did, it represented a smaller version of Jackie Robinson's integration of major-league baseball, although blacks continued to be rarities in high-level tennis.

White or black, native-born or "alien," upper-crust or aspiring, everyone behaved well on court. The peerless Tilden would throw points or even games to compensate an opponent for a bad line call. (Cynics said that, as a seven-time champion, he could afford to do so.) Applauding the other player's good shots was routine. Earl Cochell, an American top tenner, earned himself a lifetime ban from USLTA events in the 1951 Nationals by berating the umpire and referee in terms that would cause hardly a ripple today.

As the game changed socially and sartorially (long trousers faded in the late '30s), it also changed in terms of playing styles, from the McLoughlin/Tilden/Vines "cannonball" serve through the Kramer "Big Game" of serve-and-volley to the topspins of Rod Laver. Given the fast bounce of grass courts, offense almost always predominated at the Nationals. But great ground strokes, like "Little Bill" Johnston's "Western" forehand and Ken Rosewall's pinpoint backhand, still won matches.

Having made one big change—from Newport's Casino to Forest Hills' West Side club—early on, those who ran the U.S. championships during this "set" made no others of significance. After 1967, however, the biggest change of all was thrust upon them. Here and abroad, all major events became "open"—to professionals and up-front prize money. An era everyone could recognize as golden had arrived.

The Era in Pictures 1881–1967

The early years of the Newport Casino (top), where Robert Wrenn successfully defended his singles title in 1894, and the Philadelphia *Cricket Club, site of the women's championship in 1916 (above), soon give way to the West Side Tennis Club in Forest Hills, where far* *larger numbers of fans are able to watch matches like the 1925 Bill Tilden–Bill Johnston final (left), won by Tilden in five sets.*

Forest Hills becomes a showcase for the game's emerging stars like graceful Fred Perry (left), who beats Wilmer Allison 6–4, 6–3, 1–6, 8–6 for the singles title in 1934, and Helen Wills Moody (above, near court), who defeats Edith Sigourney en route to her seventh and final singles title, in 1931.

Popular Maureen Connolly (above, far court), disposing of Patricia Stewart in an early-round match, wins her third singles title in a row—and the Grand Slam—in 1953. Bobby Riggs (left) shares a celebratory moment with women's singles champion Sarah Palfrey Cooke after he has defeated Frank Kovacs 5–7, 6–1, 6–3, 6–3 for the men's title in 1941. Pancho Gonzales (right, far court) defeats Frank Parker (right, near court) in 1949 and will go on to defeat Ted Schroeder in a tough five-set final, 16–18, 2–6, 6–1, 6–2, 6–4, for his second straight singles title.

In 1962 Australian Rod Laver (left) completes the first of his two Grand Slams, defeating Roy Emerson 6–2, 6–4, 5–7, 6–4 in the final. Two of the greats in women's tennis history battle in the 1965 final as Margaret Smith (above, left) beats Billie Jean King (then Moffitt) for her second singles title. King will go on to win four herself. John Newcombe (right) wins the last men's singles title in the pre-open era, defeating Clark Graebner 6–4, 6–4, 8–6 in the 1967 final. He will win another in the open era as well.

Don Budge

If Don Budge wasn't the best player ever, he was certainly America's favorite: clean-cut, polite, an unfailing sportsman—and the winner of the only Grand Slam ever achieved by an American man. These days, only Pete Sampras has anything like Budge's appeal, or his record. The Slam, recorded in 1938, was far from serendipitous. Budge trained, practiced, and strategized for the express purpose of winning that quartet of tournaments, and he avoided the overscheduling that he had seen ruin his rivals' chances. He captured the four finals with the cumulative loss of one set—and was so thoroughly dominant that many observers thought he tossed that one to his fellow finalist and doubles partner, Gene Mako. Nineteen thirty-seven was almost as glorious for Budge: singles victories at Wimbledon and Forest Hills; the Wimbledon men's and mixed doubles, too; a dramatic, five-set win over Germany's Gottfried von Cramm to lead the U.S. into the final round of the Davis Cup. With his wavy red hair and jug ears, Budge looked rather like a caricature of a player. But his graceful athleticism and tennis physique identified him as the real item. He started out in his native Oakland, California, as a baseball player, and his left-handed batter's stance formed the basis for his backhand, generally considered the best in history. A Bunyanesque, 16.5-ounce racquet endowed every Budge shot with extra zing and forced net-rushing opponents to gamble on hitting excellent serves and approaches. Budge added a superior ability to take the ball "on the rise," a technique he learned watching Fred Perry control play against the much harder-hitting Ellsworth Vines. Mused Budge, "Suppose a man could hit the ball as hard as Vines and take it as early as Perry. Who would beat that man?" As amateur or professional, damned few, including the legendary Bill Tilden. He called Budge "the finest player 365 days a year who ever lived."

U.S. Open resume: Winner in 1937 and '38. Finalist in 1936. Also won two men's doubles titles.

Maureen Connolly

Her career flashed like a phosphorescent flare and ended, as did her life, in tragedy. But in four breathtaking seasons, from 1951 through 1954, Maureen Connolly ruled women's tennis as it has never been ruled by anyone else. She played in nine Grand Slam championships and won every one: the U.S. Nationals and Wimbledon three times each, the French twice, the Australian once. In the process, she became the first female to claim a calendar-year Grand Slam, in 1953, losing only a single set en route to those four triumphs. Her entire career, juniors included, covered a mere seven years, and when she claimed her first U.S. title, she was one month shy of her 17th birthday—the youngest winner ever until Tracy Austin eclipsed her by two months almost three decades later. "Little Mo" (as opposed to "Big Mo," the battleship) grew up in San Diego under the tennis tutelage of Eleanor "Teach" Tennant, the most famous woman coach of her time. Tennant molded Connolly's powerful, penetrating ground strokes, which she fired up by turning her hips and unleashing the full force of her stocky, 127-pound frame. With her weak serve and uncertain net game, she had to rely on "groundies," and she did so with supreme confidence. Rival Doris Hart once declared, holding thumb and forefinger an inch apart, "Maureen hits the ball this close to the lines." A cheerful, curly-haired teenager off the court, Mo was a no-nonsense woman on it: unsmiling, utterly focused, remorseless. (During a match, she said, "All I see is my opponent.") Back in San Diego after the '54 Wimbledon, she was hit by a truck while riding her horse and suffered a severely broken leg. In a foreshadowing of the Monica Seles stabbing of 1993, the traumatized Mo left her career at its peak and filed suit. She then married and had two daughters. Fifteen years later—at the age of 34, when she still could have been winning Grand Slam events—she died of cancer.

U.S. Open resume: Winner in 1951, '52, and '53. Retired in 1954 at the age of 19.

Margaret Osborne duPont

In women's doubles, before Martina, before Billie Jean, there was Margaret Osborne duPont. She and Louise Brough were the Navratilova–Shriver of their time. They owned the event at the U.S. Nationals during the 1940s, and won 12 of the 14 times they entered overall, including a stunning nine in a row. For duPont, it was actually 10; she also captured the 1941 title, with Sarah Palfrey Fabyan. The nine wins constitute merely the centerpiece of the duPont–Brough achievement. They won 20 of the 25 Grand Slam finals in which they played as a team, a record matched only by Navratilova–Shriver, three decades later. Tactically, duPont came from an era before boom-boom doubles, and she had just the shots for it. Her slice forehand kept the ball low, setting up easy winners for her team at the net. She volleyed well and played the forehand side with a special affinity for a shot that master tactician Bobby Riggs also loved: a service-return lob over the netman's head and into the server's backhand corner. A farm girl from Oregon, Osborne the tennis star married a scion of the formidable duPont clan. She won a considerable number of singles titles, too, including three at Forest Hills (1948, '49, '50), two at Stade Roland Garros, and one at Wimbledon. Brough was one of her chief rivals. They clashed in two memorable, three-set Grand Slam finals: at Wimbledon in 1949, where Brough won; and at Forest Hills in 1948, where duPont prevailed in the longest women's final ever played there. DuPont brought her skill at both singles and doubles to bear in the Wightman Cup—the annual competition between American and British players—where she rang up a perfect record (19 matches without a loss) while captaining the American side nine times. But doubles, mixed as well as women's, brought out the best in her. In the U.S. Mixed, she won a record nine times with four different partners. The last came at age 42, when old champions are normally found leafing through their clippings.

U.S. Open resume: Winner in 1948, '49, and '50. Doubles winner in 1941–1950, '55, '56, and '57.

Roy Emerson

If there were an award for Best All-Around Game, it would go to Roy Emerson. All-around in the sense not only of shots (he hit every one very well) but also of court coverage, physical fitness, and mental toughness. "Emmo," the most super-consistent of Harry Hopman's legion of Aussie champions, had everything and the record to prove it. By the time he turned pro, just before the advent of open tennis, Emerson had amassed more Grand Slam victories (26) than any male player in history, and he would add two more to his collection as a pro. They included 12 singles titles: six Australian, two each from Forest Hills, Wimbledon, and the French Open; the astonishing 16 doubles titles came with five different partners, a record at the time. His Davis Cup performance was spectacular. Joining his country's Cup squad at 17, he played on eight winning teams in nine years, going 21–2 in singles and 13–2 in doubles. In 1964, he had three legs up on a Grand Slam, losing his chance for the fourth to Nicki Pietrangeli, a clay-court specialist, in Paris. Emmo played flawlessly in both his U.S. Nationals finals, beating fellow Australians Rod Laver (7–5, 6–3, 6–2) and Fred Stolle (6–4, 6–2, 6–4) in straight sets. He was known as a prodigious beer drinker in a nation famous for them, yet he somehow managed to stay exceptionally fit for matches. A product of colorfully named Black Butt, Queensland, young Roy milked his father's cows, with two useful byproducts: milk for the family and strong wrists for the milker. At 21, on the edge of greatness but disappointed with his serve and forehand, he took a smart and unusual step: He quit the tour for an entire season and worked with Frank Sedgman, star of the previous Aussie tennis generation. Back in harness, Emerson began the process of acquiring titles that didn't stop until he did.

U.S. Open resume: Winner in 1961 and '64. Finalist in '62. All-time men's leader in Grand Slam wins with 28.

THE LEGENDS
Althea Gibson

Like baseball's Jackie Robinson, Althea Gibson will forever be remembered as much for symbol as for substance. That's inevitable. Not only was she the first black person to play in the U.S. championships, she also made a Cinderella ascent from tattered overalls to tennis dresses. Born into a family of South Carolina cotton farmers, she was raised on the mean streets of Harlem, which she roamed, she recalled, "as a vagabond." Her father, by then a garage mechanic, had fantastic notions of her becoming a boxer. But Althea took up tennis. She caught the eye of two prominent officials of the historically black American Tennis Association, and they arranged for her—as one of them later did for Arthur Ashe—to live in a nurturing, tennis-oriented household and travel the ATA circuit. Carefully managed by the ATA, she gradually worked her way into mainstream tournaments. But aside from the everyday slights black people endured in 1940s America, she collided with an odd socio-athletic wall: Grass-court events, her entree to Forest Hills, were played only at country clubs, where "colored" were not welcome. She nonetheless ascended, again gradually, to the hallowed West Side Tennis Club, "where all I thought about was, How am I going to play this game and win?" Five-foot-11, strong, and fluid, Gibson won plenty. She was a hard server and fearless attacker, so confident of her volley that she often came to net when her opponent was already there. At Forest Hills in 1957, after losing in the final the previous year, Gibson captured the title with a 6–3, 6–2 victory over Louise Brough. She won again in 1958, beating Darlene Hard 3–6, 6–1, 6–2 to become the queen of U.S. tennis. After a fling at pro tennis (then in its infancy for women), Gibson turned to golf and played that professionally, too. She never did become a boxer.

U.S. Open resume: Winner in 1957 and '58. Finalist in 1956.

Pancho Gonzales

When Ricardo Alonso Gonzales reached Forest Hills, right after World War II, big time tennis had seen a few social—shall we say—wild cards, but no card as wild as "Pancho." Not only was he working class, he was also Mexican-American—and a school truant (which kept him from competing in Los Angeles–area tournaments as a youngster). Gonzales never developed much in the way of social graces, and he could be positively truculent toward officials, sponsors, and the like. His marvelous game trumped all of those disqualifications. Some rate it the best ever. He served so well that Jack Kramer, who saw virtually all the greats and faced Gonzales over and over again as a pro, ranks his first serve the most consistently excellent and his second among the four best. His first serves were astonishingly reliable in clutch situations: Kramer's stats on Gonzales for one year showed 87 percent of first balls in play on break points. Eventually, Gonzales's serve indoors became all but unbreakable. The rest of his game was a clever mixture of pace and quasi-junk, and he moved and defended well. He rose through the crowd faster than anyone before him and without professional coaching: Eastern grass-court debut in 1947, U.S. singles winner the very next year. After repeating as champion in '49, he went for the gold as a pro. Too soon, as it turned out. Both the Gonzales game and personality were still immature, and Kramer flattened him repeatedly. Again, Pancho developed very rapidly, and over the next decade, he fended off a string of big-name challengers, winning the U.S. Pro singles a record seven consecutive times. He continued playing, and often winning, right on into the open era. In 1969, at 41, he defeated Charlie Pasarell, two decades his junior, in the then-longest match in Wimbledon history, a 112-game marathon.

U.S. Open resume: Winner in 1948 and '49. Turned pro in 1950 and thus was ineligible to compete until the open era.

THE LEGENDS
Jack Kramer

Big Jack (or Jake) invented the "Big Game." Athough there had been serve-and-volleyers before him, the crew-cut Kramer pioneered the S-and-V version we see today. In fact, he virtually codified it: Serve to the backhand; attack on your own and the other guy's second serve; get to the net on every big point; go with your strength, even if it means hitting into his strength. Huge first deliveries were less important than medium-paced, accurate slices followed by well-placed first volleys. Throw in a Big Bertha forehand, which he also possessed, and you had a hell of an attack. Kramer learned the Big Game basics as a teenager at the Los Angeles Tennis Club, where he picked up matches with many of the best players of the period. He perfected his system upon turning pro in 1947. By that time he had become the dominant force in amateur tennis, a two-time winner at Forest Hills, a Wimbledon champion, and key man on the U.S. squad that captured the first post-war Davis Cup in Australia. (The Wimbledon title, in '47, came with the loss of only 37 games in seven matches, a record.) As a fledgling pro, Kramer faced the reigning champ, Bobby Riggs. Opening night, played in Madison Square Garden as a blizzard buried New York City, turned out to be Riggs's high point. He beat Kramer then, but Jake went on to vanquish him, 69 matches to 20, in the grinding series of one-night stands that constituted the pro tour. When the next hot amateur, Pancho Gonzales, replaced the veteran Riggs, Kramer handled him with even greater ease. The last and final victim was Aussie Frank Sedgman. Then, plagued by an aching back, Big Jack became Big [tour] Promoter as well as TV analyst and all-around tennis sage. He also became politically controversial, wrangling publicly with Billie Jean King and others over parity in prize money for women and men.

U.S. Open resume: Winner in 1946 and '47 before becoming the dominant player on the professional tour.

Alice Marble

A man's game in women's clothing ... Jack Kramer's female counterpart. Those are only two descriptions that could be applied to Alice Marble, the blonde attacker from California. Marble, declared Billie Jean King, "played tennis as no woman had before her. She could hit every shot in the game—with power." Marble won four U.S. championships and a flock of other titles in the years immediately before World War II, and she did it despite illnesses and two untimely breaks in her career. Like so many other top American women players, Marble rode out of the Far West to conquer the East and beyond. Five-feet-seven, 140 pounds, and notably strong, she had an all-court, offensive game that took women's tennis to the next level and encouraged the development of similar players who followed her over the next three decades. She volleyed very well and served even better—better, some say, than any woman who had preceded her. Although far from the on-court glamour girl that Gussy Moran became a decade later, Marble had no compunctions about flouting the tradition of demure and dowdy tennis fashions, often wearing short-sleeved shirts and the shortest shorts yet seen on the circuit. In 1933 and again the following year, she collapsed during matches; after the second incident, which was variably attributed to pleurisy or tuberculosis, doctors said she would never play again. She not only played but also won, in fact, ascending to the zenith of a highly successful career that would include a lock on the U.S. championships, where she took the women's singles, doubles, and mixed doubles titles three years in a row. Ten years after winning her last major title, Marble proved herself a champion of a different kind. She befriended and publicly supported Althea Gibson when Gibson was struggling to become the first black woman to compete at Forest Hills. When Gibson left the court after winning her first-round match, a smiling Alice Marble was at her side.

U.S. Open resume: Winner in 1936, '38, '39, and '40. Also won four women's and four mixed doubles titles.

THE LEGENDS
Fred Perry

No one has ever cut a more commanding figure on court than Britain's Fred Perry. With his chiseled good looks, athletic physique, and immaculately combed hair, he was so much the classic tennis ideal that his eventual marketing of a clothing line seemed a most natural enterprise. How ironic, then, that Perry arose not from his country's tennis-minded gentry but from the working class. (His father was a textile mill worker and Labor Party M.P.) Even during his greatest years, there was class friction between Perry and the gentlemen who oversaw his own nation's championship, Wimbledon. Perry specialized in "first and last since" distinctions. When he won Wimbledon in 1934, he became the first (and last) Englishman to do so since 1909; and in capturing Forest Hills in 1933, the first (and last) since 1903. His game was rooted in a driving forehand, which he hit best on the run and with a wrist snap that no coach would ever try to teach. He coupled the forehand with the difficult technique of hitting on the rise—what baseball calls the short hop. Perry perfected that style—which John McEnroe employed four decades later—during six months of practice in the winter of 1929–30. It helped Perry play aggressively and left opponents with a discomforting split second less to prepare for his shot. In addition, he moved quickly and tirelessly, calling on reflexes sharpened by his pre-tennis days as a top-level table tennis player (he won a world championship). Perry relied on fitness and mental toughness to pull out grinding, five-set matches. He also had another, less-heroic side. In an impeccably sporting era, Perry was a devoted and unapologetic practitioner of gamesmanship: comments and other ploys, oncourt and off, to gain a psychological edge. "Fred," wrote Ted Tinling, a longtime friend, "never missed a trick when it came to the psychology of winning."

U.S. Open resume: Winner in 1933, '34, and '36.

Bobby Riggs

It is Bobby Riggs's fate to be remembered by the broad tennis public more as a hustler and jester than as a player. That's justified in the sense that he courted his reputation, but totally unjust to his tennis abilities. People who know the game and saw Riggs at his peak rank him among the best half-dozen players of all time. Scrawny, funny-looking Bobby? The guy who handicapped himself in crazy ways to win bets with suckers? The blatant self-promoting sexist who crumpled in his big match against Billie Jean King? The very same. There was a time—an era—in both amateur and pro tennis when Riggs represented the highest order of playing skill. It began in 1936, when he won the U.S clay court doubles, and continued into 1973, when, at age 55, he made Margaret Smith Court look as outclassed as he himself proceeded to look against King. Along the way, Riggs won Wimbledon, two U.S. Nationals, and two Professional Championships. In his Wimbledon year, he also captured both the men's and mixed doubles for a rare hat trick. Riggs possessed one all-time great shot, the lob—appropriate for a defensive specialist. But he played defense as though it were a form of offense: masterful ball placement, maddening angles and dinks, a forehand that stood up to almost anyone else's, and a serve that made up in precision and variety what it lacked in pace. "Nobody could outsteady or outthink Bobby," one contemporary wrote, adding that "he was never out of the match until the last point was over." When Riggs faced Jack Kramer's new version of serve-and-volley on the pro tour, he abruptly changed his own game, following his serve consistently and successfully to net. As a pro, Riggs gave Kramer all he could handle and narrowly beat Don Budge. No mere jester could have come close to doing either.

U.S. Open resume: Winner in 1939 and '41. Finalist in 1940.

Bill Talbert & Gardnar Mulloy

We saw great teams before they began, we've seen probably greater ones (McEnroe–Fleming, Hewitt–McMillan) since they've left. But Talbert and Mulloy were doubles at the championship level in a way no other teams have ever been. In their era together, which stretched across 12 years of finals at Forest Hills, their names were virtually synonymous with the team game. And each won numerous major tournaments with other partners: Talbert (on right in photo below), the National mixed doubles four years running with Margaret Osborne; Mulloy, the Wimbledon doubles (at the hoary age of 43) with Budge Patty. (It can be argued that the Mulloy–Talbert star descended just in time to avoid facing the powerful Australian teams of the 1950s.) The tall, rangy "Gar," a Miami product, captured his first national title—in a father-and-son event—in 1939 and reached his last Forest Hills final in 1957. Cincinnati-bred "Billy" was a lifelong diabetic who said he pursued tennis partly to prove that people with that affliction could succeed—and partly to rise above his Depression-ridden beginnings. Talbert used his tennis skills deftly to rise in social circles and the New York business world, becoming, as sociologist E. Digby Baltzell put it, "a Brooks Brothers gent *par excellence*." Although neither man achieved stardom in singles, each scored notable singles successes: Mulloy was ranked No. 1 in the U.S. in 1952; Talbert was an American top tenner 13 times between 1941 and 1954. As a pair, their hallmarks were faultless strategy and the kind of teamwork that comes only from countless matches and an innate sense of what makes doubles a very different game. Talbert's book *The Game of Doubles in Tennis* remains the most serious, complex study of the subject ever written.

U.S. Open resume: Doubles winners in 1942, '45, '46, and '48. Finalists in 1950 and '53.

Bill Tilden

Forty-four years after his death and almost 70 after his last U.S. Nationals title, Bill Tilden still commands much support as the best player of all time. Just the highlights of his career border on the fabulous: world No. 1 for an unmatched six years; a record seven singles championships (within a 10-year span) at the Nationals; three at Wimbledon (where he seldom competed); a professional career that spanned two decades and virtually created the pro enterprise. Tall, slender, and elegant, with a flair for the dramatic, he dominated every scene. As Fred Perry, himself a matinee idol, put it, "When Tilden walked on the court, he was the king." Not at the outset. Tilden labored in the game's middle ranks until goaded by a Forest Hills loss to Bill Johnston, who picked on his weak backhand. Tilden went straightaway to Providence, Rhode Island, where he worked for an entire winter perfecting his backhand. "Big Bill" dominated "Little Bill" thereafter, beating him in four consecutive Forest Hills finals. Tilden mastered every stroke: cannonball and "kick" serve, forehand and backhand, drop shot and lob, spins of every sort; and he deployed them all with the skill of a chess Grand Master. Even more, he mastered psychology and strategy, concentrating on what he called "break[ing] up the other man's game." Mused Rene Lacoste, "Tilden always seems to have a thousand means of putting the ball away from his opponent's reach. . . . Even when beaten, he always leaves an impression on the public mind that he was superior to the victor." Those two qualities, the one talent, the other alchemy, made Tilden the first and greatest international tennis celebrity. He played that role relentlessly, consorting with the glitterati and spending his winnings lavishly. In a less tolerant era, accusations of homosexuality eventually brought him down. He died in a run-down Los Angeles apartment, packed, dressed, and ready to compete—at the age of 60—in the U.S. Pro Championships.

U.S. Open resume: Winner in 1920, '21, '22, '23, '24, '25, and '29.

THE LEGENDS
Ellsworth Vines

"His serve and forehand," says Sidney Wood, "could shock a seismograph." Wood, a top player throughout the 1930s, is talking about Ellsworth Vines. The tall, slender Californian was the phenomenon of the early '30s. He competed as a touring amateur for only five years, yet during that period and a few campaigns as a professional, established himself among the best male players ever. His game was power—with a sartorial flair. Jack Kramer, perhaps aided by Frank Deford, his amanuensis, described Vines as "dressed like Fred Astaire and hitting shots like Babe Ruth." Kramer ranked Vines's natural ability with that of Lew Hoad and Rod Laver, saying: "When Elly was on, you'd be lucky to get your racquet on the ball once you served it." Many of Vines's contemporaries agreed: If Elly was hot, little could be done to stop him. After Vines had demolished Britain's Bunny Austin in the '32 Wimbledon final, Austin said of the match-ending ace that he didn't know whether the ball had gone by him on the right or the left. Serves, like forehands, were hit almost perfectly flat, with no speed-reducing (and cautionary) spin. On tour in a 39-match series, Vines reportedly averaged an incredible 2.4 aces per service game—against Don Budge, the finest player of his era. Even against run-of-the-draw competition, today's acemeister, Goran Ivanisevic, has never equaled that. Vines's compact amateur record: 1931—U.S. singles; 1932—U.S. and Wimbledon singles, U.S. doubles; 1933—Australian doubles, U.S. mixed doubles. With his power game, grass was obviously his surface; yet he also won both singles and doubles titles at the U.S. national clay-court tournament. While still a formidable player, Vines abandoned tennis and turned to golf—pro golf. He starred there, too, reaching the semifinals of the 1951 PGA Championship.

U.S. Open resume: Winner in 1931 and '32. Also won one men's title and one mixed doubles title.

Helen Wills

When does unbeatable become untouchable? When you play seven straight years on the tour *without losing a set*. That's what Helen Wills did between 1927 and 1933, a period that saw her win 158 matches and 27 tournaments. That stretch of tournaments included four U.S. singles titles to add to the three she'd won earlier. As great as she was, Wills played second violin to the tennis prima donna of the era, Suzanne Lenglen. Their records were comparable, but France's Lenglen exhibited panache on and off court, while America's Wills had such a bland personality that sportswriter Grantland Rice dubbed her "Little Miss Poker Face." Because Lenglen turned pro when Wills was just hitting her stride, the two met only once in a singles match: in 1926 in Cannes, France. Amid huge hoopla and horrendous line calls, *la Grande Suzanne* won 6–3, 8–6 (whereupon she collapsed on a bench and wept). Wills was more attractive than Lenglen, and she had her own trademark: a white visor invariably worn during matches. But she had no time for tears and little for smiles. ("The secret of mirth," she once said cryptically, "is to keep it secret.") All that charmed the public to a degree; but later she became altogether too regal to attract more than respect. As a 14-year-old learning the game in Berkeley, California, Wills caught the eye of Hazel Wightman, sponsor of the Wightman Cup. A mere six weeks of work, it is said, transformed the youngster into national girls champion. Two years after that she was in the finals at Forest Hills. Wills's game had its limits. She hit cross-court incessantly, and she didn't move well. But she was strong and fit, had a fine slice serve, and really pounded her ground strokes. Above all, she concentrated. As she said in her autobiography, "I had one thought, and that was to put the ball across the net."

U.S. Open resume: Winner in 1923, '24, '25, '27, '28, '29, and '31.

SECOND SET: THE OPEN

KODES 46621
NEWCOMBE 61462

ERA IN FOREST HILLS 1968–1977

The women had their dual championships, too, with little difference from a quality standpoint between the amateur and pro versions: Margaret Smith Court and Virginia Wade the respective victors, Maria Bueno and Billie Jean King the respective vanquished. Ominously, from the perspective of tranquility on the tour, Wade's reward for winning amounted to less than half of Okker's for losing. Her opponent that day, the ever-feisty King, would soon lead a largely successful crusade for gender parity.

Money issues aside, this was a magnificent era in women's tennis, with the top echelon richer in talent, potential, and stirring rivalries than ever before. Nineteen seventy-four alone displayed this quartet of Hall of Famers, each at or close to the top of her game: King, Wade, Evonne Goolagong, and Chris Evert. Now a maturing champion rather than the demure "Chrissie" of a few years earlier, Evert was poised for her greatest sustained run. By the end of 1977, she would win three U.S. Opens, two Wimbledons, two French Opens, and two Italian Opens—in all, 55 of the 76 tournaments and 339 of the 361 matches she played.

The change to Har-Tru courts at the Open obviously helped Evert, whose ground strokes remained by far her principal weapons. But clay was hardly the key: when the Open moved to Flushing Meadows's hard courts, she won three times there; and singles victories on grass at both Wimbledon and the Australian Open remained in her future.

Yet the match from this era that many Evert fans remember best took place back in the 1971 Open, against Mary Ann Eisel in the second round. Eisel was a good grass-court player. She won a close first set against the 16-year-old backcourter and proceeded to 6–5, 40–love—triple match point—in the second. How did Evert react? She simply hit two clean winners off Eisel's serve, received the gift of a double fault, then survived three more match points in that game alone. She went on to win the tiebreak easily and the third set more easily still.

When Evert and Jimmy Connors, her counterpart

Writing in *Sports Illustrated*, Kim Chapin offered a thoughtful explanation of the pros' collapse: They "play in their own little world—mostly indoors—and seem less adaptable to change than the amateurs." In addition, the pros were vulnerable to ambush by loosey-goosey, make-my-reputation amateurs of whom they'd barely heard, let alone played against. But all that was a fleeting phenomenon. Soon Laver, Rosewall, et al. would again be doing what they did so well—winning.

phenom among the men, got engaged in late 1973, it literally thrilled the tennis world. Even hardened sportswriters, particularly those at the British tabloids, burbled about the "lovebird double" and coined similarly inspired phrases. When the birds both won at Wimbledon in 1974—a 33–1 parlay, according to London bookies—the romantics' cup overflowed. (Unfortunately, or fortunately, the engagement proved short-lived.)

This would be Connors's greatest Grand Slam year, with titles at each of the three events he played (he did not go to the French). At the U.S. Open, although weakened by a virus infection, he raced through the field to the final. There he all but humiliated Rosewall, losing a mere two games and spending a scant 68 minutes to become the youngest Forest Hills men's champion since Rosewall himself 18 years earlier. Connors declined to patronize his opponent. Asked if he pitied the elder statesman while demolishing him, Jimbo replied, "I've seen people pity

CLASSIC MATCHES

1974 FINAL:
BILLIE JEAN KING VERSUS
EVONNE GOOLAGONG

To the sellout crowd, the King–Goolagong classic was especially welcome because it came on the heels of Jimmy Connors's lightning-speed victory over Ken Rosewall in the other final. King, who felt she'd "started to go downhill" at that point, later called this "the best match the two of us have ever played." Goolagong was primed for it. The day before she had ended Chris Evert's 55-match victory streak, winning the opening set at love. She again started brilliantly, pounding backhand passing shots to take the opening set by 6–3. King stuck with her usual aggressive game, and Goolagong, a streaky player, lost enough of her edge to reverse the first-set score. In the third, Goolagong raced off to another big lead, but King kept fighting for every point. One exchange saw her fend off good Goolagong passing shots on either side, then drill a winning volley off a ball hit hard and directly at her. King clawed back to 5–all, then simply took over, surrendering a single point in the last two games. Said the exultant victor: "How did I win? I don't have a clue."

1968 FINAL:
ARTHUR ASHE VERSUS TOM OKKER

The first U.S. Open paid out $100,000 in prize money, but the singles winner, Arthur Ashe, came away with nothing but expenses. Ashe was in the army and therefore an amateur who could collect only $20 per day. He didn't much mind: This was his first Grand Slam title—satisfaction enough at that point—and over-the-table payments were very much a novelty. Ashe not only became the last amateur to win the U.S. championship, he also became the first (and so far only) black man to do so. A match pregnant with such historic possibilities should have drawn an overflow crowd. But perhaps because it was postponed by rain, the final filled little more than half of the Forest Hills stadium. Ashe's power and sometimes-brilliant shotmaking were pitted against Okker's speed and agility. Predictably on a grass surface, power won, but not before Okker had pushed matters to their five-set limit. Rallies were few. Ashe blasted 26 aces, volleyed well, and often seemed at the point of finishing the match. Yet Okker repeatedly scrambled back, aided by his opponent's frequent lapses. Ashe broke serve early in the fifth set but had to sweat out a couple of poor service games of his own in order to hold the break. Hold it he did, then served out the 5–3 game at love. For once, vanquished seemed as happy as victor: Okker carried off $14,000, a big haul in that faraway tennis time.

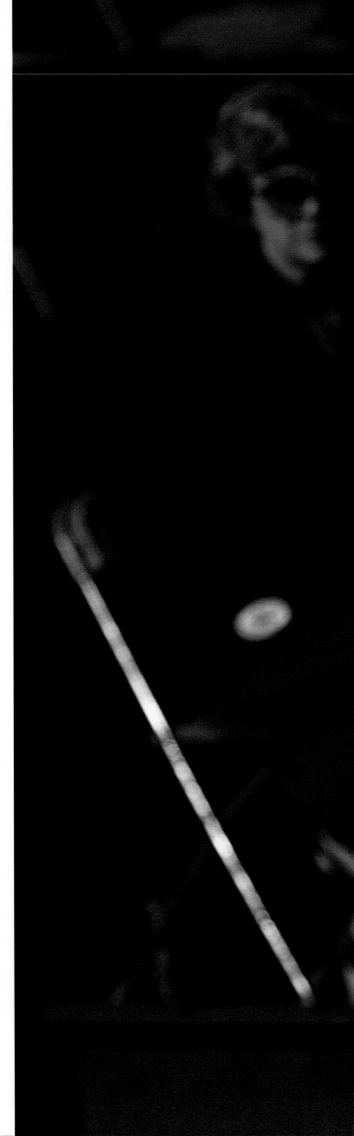

Ken Rosewall and then see him win 6–3 in the fifth."

Although Rosewall emphatically ran out of geriatric miracles at the '74 Open, he nonetheless, in 1970, managed to cap his own grand moments at Forest Hills. That year, at age 35, "Muscles," as his Aussie chums called him, defeated one of them, Tony Roche. The victory came 14 years after Rosewall's first U.S. title. Not even Bill Tilden could come close to matching such a span of success.

No major racial issues complicated the progress of this "set." Gender issues did: not only parity in prize money but also transsexuality (what would Richard Sears and his Boston brahmins have thought?). The person in question was Renée Richards, née Richard Raskind. I had a slight connection to her more prosaic past. Raskind had been Yale's No. 1 when the Elis played the Amherst team for which I labored somewhere down the line. He'd gone on to compete at Forest Hills and Wimbledon.

In 1975, after "sex reassignment" surgery, Raskind began a new life, and ophthalmologic practice, in Southern California as Renée Richards. She also began playing women's tournaments and eventually applied to compete in the U.S. Open. Bitter debate followed, with the Women's Tennis Association opposing her application. Richards sued and won a court order to play the 1977 event. Although she was a good serve-and-volleyer, this was clay; besides, she drew Virginia Wade in the first round. A sort of half-battle of the sexes ensued, and Wade, like King against Bobby Riggs, emerged the winner.

Since money lingers on most of our minds, let us note that it took U.S. Open officials only six years to rectify the injustice done singles champion Wade at the outset of open tennis. In 1973, Margaret Smith Court and John Newcombe each received $25,000 for winning their respective events, the first time in the sport's major tournament history that prize money was awarded equally. Twenty-five grand may seem like chump change to this year's Open winners, but back then it bought a lot of baubles—or Fosters.

The Era in Pictures 1968–1977

As in the society at large, 1968 is a historic year for tennis, as Arthur Ashe (above) becomes the first black man to win a tennis major in the very first U.S. championship open to both amateurs and pros. Ashe defeats Holland's Tom Okker in a grueling five-setter that includes an opening-set 14–12 victory for Ashe. In the women's draw another elegant and popular champion emerges as Britain's Virginia Wade (left) upsets Billie Jean King for the title.

1970

CHAMPIONS

SINGLES
Ken Rosewall
Margaret Smith Court

DOUBLES
Pierre Barthes
& Nikki Pilic

Margaret Smith Court
& Judy Dalton

MIXED DOUBLES
Margaret Smith Court
& Marty Riessen

Margaret Smith Court (above) has an amazing tournament, completing a Grand Slam by defeating Rosie Casals, then going on to win both the women's doubles title (with Judy Dalton) and the mixed doubles title (with Marty Riessen). Ken Rosewall (right) wins the men's title, defeating Tony Roche in a final that includes the first use of the newly instituted tiebreaker. It is Rosewall's second U.S. title, and it comes a remarkable 14 years after his first.

1971

CHAMPIONS

SINGLES
Stan Smith
Billie Jean King

DOUBLES
John Newcombe
& Roger Taylor

Rosie Casals
& Judy Dalton

MIXED DOUBLES
Billie Jean King
& Owen Davidson

"I like demonstrative crowds. People who pay their hard-earned money for a ticket ought to be able to make noise. Maybe the girls could wear earmuffs."

—Billie Jean King

Backhanded complement: A pair of Americans take home the singles titles for the first time since 1955 as Billie Jean King (above) defeats Rosie Casals 6–4, 7–6 in the Forest Hills final, and Stan Smith (left) takes a four-setter from Jan Kodes, 3–6, 6–3, 6–2, 7–6. Smith never appears in an Open singles final again but will win a total of four doubles titles with partner Bob Lutz.

"This is a great player. And when he brushes up on his court manners he will be even better."

—Arthur Ashe on Ilie Nastase

1972

CHAMPIONS

SINGLES
Ilie Nastase
Billie Jean King

DOUBLES
Cliff Drysdale
& Roger Taylor

Françoise Durr
& Betty Stove

MIXED DOUBLES
Margaret Smith Court
& Marty Riessen

The tempestuous, wily and unpredictable Ilie Nastase (left) uses his astonishing assortment of shots to win his first Open, defeating Arthur Ashe in five sets. In the process he battles back from a breakpoint, down 1–3 in the fourth set. In the women's draw Billie Jean King (above) sprints to the third of her four singles titles by defeating Kerry Melville in the final, 6–3, 7–5.

1973

CHAMPIONS

SINGLES
John Newcombe
Margaret Smith Court

DOUBLES
Owen Davidson
& John Newcombe

Margaret Smith Court
& Virginia Wade

MIXED DOUBLES
Billie Jean King
& Owen Davidson

Evonne Goolagong (above), the epitome of oncourt grace, makes the first of four consecutive losing appearances in the Forest Hills final, falling in a close match to Margaret *Smith Court, 6–7, 7–5, 2–6. Australia's John Newcombe (right, near court) takes his second U.S. championship, outlasting Jan Kodes 6–4, 1–6, 4–6, 6–2, 6–3, in the final.*

While Billie Jean King (above) is performing the expected by defeating Evonne Goolagong for her fourth singles title, there is a new sensation by the name of

Jimmy Connors (right) dominating the men's draw. In the final, the 22-year-old Connors shows absolutely no respect for his elders, disposing of the 39-year-old Ken

Rosewall 6–1, 6–0, 6–1 for the most dominant victory in the history of the U.S. men's finals. It is the first of five straight trips to the final for Connors.

1974

"The best tennis of my life, all 22 years of it. I didn't miss a ball." —Jimmy Connors

1975

CHAMPIONS

SINGLES
Manuel Orantes
Chris Evert

DOUBLES
Ilie Nastase
& Jimmy Connors

Margaret Smith Court
& Virginia Wade

MIXED DOUBLES
Rosie Casals
& Dick Stockton

"I didn't believe that it would be possible for him to hit passing shots and play like he did all the way through. But unfortunately for me, he did."

—Jimmy Connors on Manuel Orantes

The combustible combination of Ilie Nastase (far left) and Jimmy Connors (left, above) catches fire in the doubles draw as the pair defeats Tom Okker and Marty Riessen in straight sets for the title. In the men's singles competition Manuel Orantes (above) thrills one of the Open's first night-time crowds by coming back from five match points to defeat Guillermo Vilas in the semis before upsetting defending champ Connors in the final.

"Borg, he is
different story.
You look on his
face for emotion
and there is
nothing."

—Manuel Orantes

CHAMPIONS

SINGLES
Jimmy Connors
Chris Evert

DOUBLES
Marty Riessen
& Tom Okker

Delina Boshoff
& Ilana Kloss

MIXED DOUBLES
Billie Jean King
& Phil Dent

The unflappable Bjorn Borg (left), fresh off a victory at Wimbledon, makes the first of his four fruitless trips to the Open final, falling to Jimmy Connors in an exhausting four-set match that includes a 7–6 (11–9) victory for Connors in the third set. Chris Evert (above, right) wins the women's title, defeating Evonne Goolagong (above, left) easily in the final for the second straight year. It is the second of four consecutive U.S. Open singles titles for Evert.

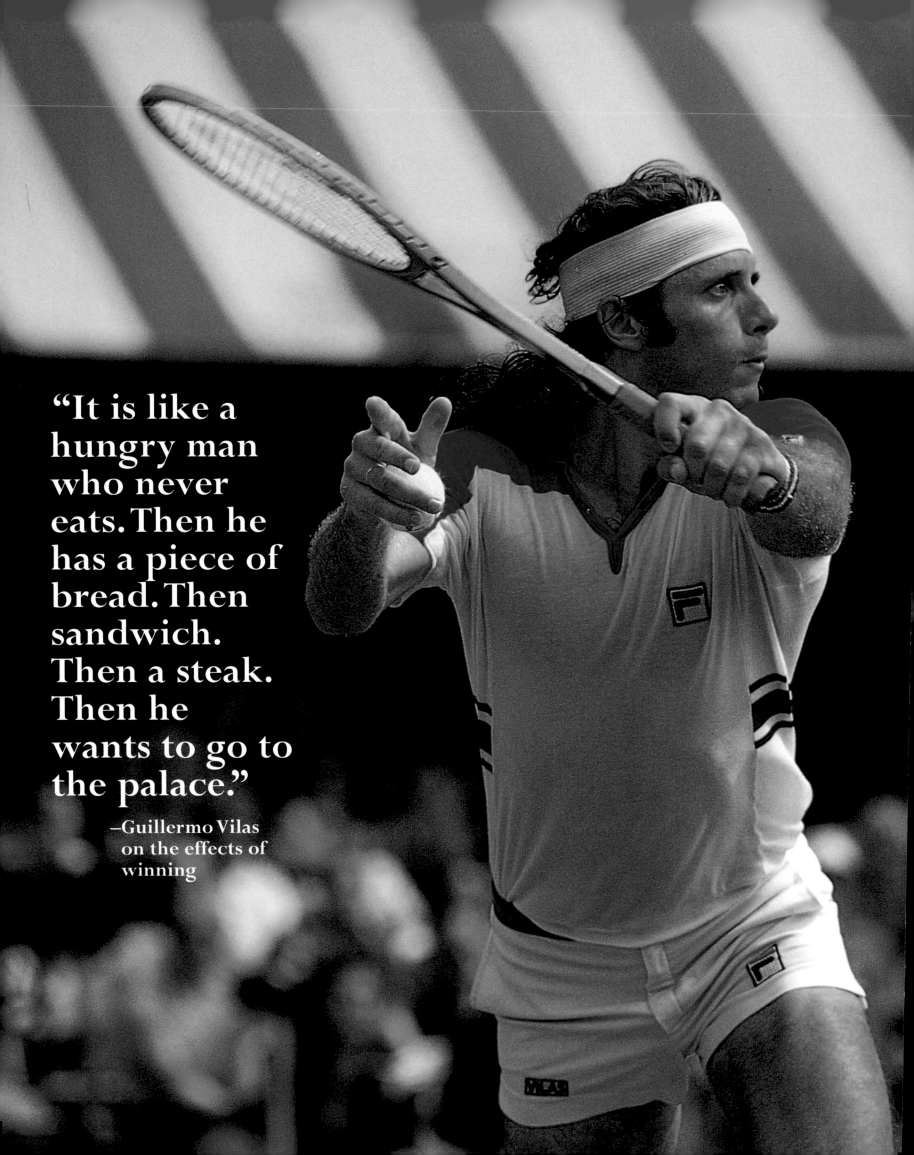

"It is like a hungry man who never eats. Then he has a piece of bread. Then sandwich. Then a steak. Then he wants to go to the palace."

—Guillermo Vilas
on the effects of
winning

1977

As the tournament says farewell to Forest Hills, Guillermo Vilas (left) pulls off a major Open upset, defeating Jimmy Connors 2–6, 6–3, 7–6, 6–0 in the final.

Chris Evert (above) takes her third straight singles title by defeating Wendy Turnbull in straight sets. The tennis world is beginning to wonder whether

a challenger will ever emerge for Evert, failing to notice a Czech defector named Martina Navratilova who is waiting in the wings.

THE LEGENDS
Arthur Ashe

Whenever one talks about Arthur Ashe, the instinct is to extol his astuteness, humanity, simple decency, range of interests and talents, and, of course, his personal courage. Ashe the man has largely supplanted Ashe the tennis player. Perhaps that's as it should be. But there's a lot to admire, to savor, about Ashe the player, too.

Inevitably, even his tennis exploits tend to be clothed in racial and social significance: first black man to win a major championship, hold the top American ranking, or become a certified star in the sport; low-key but resolute proponent of attracting minorities to tennis; dependable advocate of balancing principle and good sense on such issues as playing for, or boycotting, the U.S. Davis Cup team.

But in purely tennis terms, two memories of Ashe—one a quality, the other a specific match—come immediately to mind. The quality was his relaxed, go-for-broke style of play. Ashe was a pure hitter—like many others but with a lot more talent than they possessed. Yet he liked to dink and feather the ball, too. No matter the choice, he always went for the shot, as tennis players say, that made for short points and flocks of outright winners and outright losers.

"When you're confident," he would tell himself, "you can do anything." He was seldom less than confident. And he once told writer John McPhee, "I hate orderliness." His game was disorderly beauty.

Except once, in that most memorable of Ashe matches: the Wimbledon final, 1975. The opponent: James Scott Connors. Jimbo owned Wimbledon in those days. In the '74 final, he had demolished Ken Rosewall. He was No. 1 in the world, at the peak of his great career, and he'd had a fine '74–75 campaign. Ashe, by comparison, was just shy of 32, sixth-seeded in the singles, a 10–1 bookies' underdog.

What followed was one of the towering tennis upsets. Ashe engineered it by changing his tennis nature as well as his tennis style. He set aside the flat-out, hit-for-winners game plan that grass favored and which came so naturally to him it hardly *was* a plan. In its place, he substituted a chesslike, thinking-man's game full of clever spins, alternating speeds, and low shots that had Connors scooping and digging out balls when he wanted to smash them. Ashe won in four sets. It proved to be his only Wimbledon title in any category.

In fact, Ashe won few other Grand Slam events: the Australian singles and doubles; the French doubles; and the U.S. singles in 1968, the first

> "Ashe the man has largely supplanted Ashe the tennis player. Perhaps that's as it should be. But there's a lot to admire, to savor, about Ashe the player, too."

year of open tennis. That victory was over Dutchman Tom Okker, and the open situation provided a strange twist: Ashe played as an amateur (a lieutenant in the Army), Okker as a pro. Ashe prevailed in five nerve-wracking sets, on the strength of 26 aces and lots of punishing service returns. His amateur status restricted his financial payoff to some $20 a day in expense money.

Nineteen sixty-eight was Ashe's year in Davis Cup, too. He won 11 straight singles matches as the U.S. squad regained (from Australia) the prize that had evaded it for the previous four years. Black militants had hounded him to quit "Whitey's" Davis Cup team. He ignored them, not because he didn't care but because he flatly disagreed. Tennis was his game. By playing it well and with dignity, he knew, he could do much more for his race and for America than by not playing at all.

U.S. Open resume: Winner in 1968. Finalist in 1972.

Margaret Smith Court

If she had stayed faithfully with the tour, Margaret Smith Court would almost surely rank as the greatest female player. She quit to get married and had two year-long absences and a couple of other brief "retirements." In addition, she played her last years as the mother of a child and one (losing) Wimbledon final when pregnant. Distractions notwithstanding, only a single player of either gender, Martina Navratilova, rivals Court in total Grand Slam tournament victories in all events combined—in Court's case, 62.

Her Grand Slam record is stunning in both numbers and scope. Court won every kind of event in every Slam venue: in singles, five U.S. championships, three Wimbledons, five French, 11 Australians; and dozens of doubles titles. In Federation Cup play, her singles tally was 22–0; against Billie Jean King, a legend in her own right, a commanding 22–10. En route to that record, she became the second woman (after Maureen Connolly) to capture the Grand Slam.

Further, when Court reached a Slam final, she was virtually certain to emerge the winner. Of the 29 in which she played, she lost only five, a big-encounter success rate that invites comparison with the old New York Yankees. None of those Court wins surpassed one she rang up over King at Wimbledon in her Grand Slam year, 1970. The score (in that pre-tiebreak era) was a nerve-stretching 14–12, 11–9. Both players competed despite painful disabilities: Court, an ankle injury so severe she'd taken shots for it from the quarterfinals on; King, an injured knee that caused her leg to cramp and prevented her from following her serve to the net late in the match.

Not so dramatic, but very impressive from the standpoint of the surface involved, was Court's victory over Chris Evert in the final of the 1973 French Open. Although a newcomer as a full-time tour player, Evert would win 88 of 98 matches that year. She was already a terror on the surface she would eventually own—clay—and three years earlier, as a high school sophomore, she had actually beaten Court at a small event in North Carolina. Yet when big chips were down, on the *terre battue* ("beaten earth") in Paris, Court prevailed in three close sets.

Court accomplished all that despite a confessed problem with nerves—and an early, forced switching of hands. Like Connolly, she was a natural southpaw taught to play tennis with her right hand. When she quit high school to concentrate on the sport, a wealthy Melbourne businessman not only paid for her lessons but also sent her to what used to be called charm school. Court turned out to be modest, straightforward, and devoutly religious.

Among the women of her era, nobody hit the ball

"Her Grand Slam record is stunning in both numbers and scope. Court won every kind of event in every Slam venue...."

as hard as Court. She had natural physical strength, and she developed it assiduously while working hard to stay in top shape. Given those attributes, she played aggressively—"like a man," in the meant-to-be-complimentary phrase of the day. Court attacked off both sides and on her serve. Her success at volleying owed much to her long reach (King called her "the Arm").

Near the end of her career, Court played the patsy in the first of Bobby Riggs's famous inter-gender exhibitions. In light of her skills, power, and relative youth, she should have beaten the 55-year-old hustler. But Riggs, a consummate match player when money was at stake, dinked, angled, and sliced her to death, and she assured her own downfall by succumbing to nerves and performing very poorly.

The high point of Court's day was a post-match comment: "I didn't expect so many soft shots. We girls don't play like that."

U.S. Open resume: Winner in 1962, '65, '69, '70, and '73. Also won five women's and eight mixed doubles titles.

THE LEGENDS
Evonne Goolagong

Although she did not win the U.S. Open, Evonne Goolagong deserves legendary status because of her four consecutive trips to the singles finals, her ethnic background, and especially her uniquely graceful style of play. Goolagong was part Australian aborigine, a group that historically has had to struggle to achieve recognition in any of Australia's "majority" enterprises, including tennis.

Those who do achieve in such situations usually benefit from a strong helping hand. In the case of young Evonne, born to a dirt-poor sheepshearer, that hand belonged to a Sydney teaching pro named Vic Edwards. Impressed with the 13-year-old's natural ability, especially her ease of movement, Edwards offered to have her live with his family while he coached her. Her parents gave their blessing. From that humble start, Evonne developed rapidly into a first-rate player.

In 1971, only her second year on the tour, she won both the French and Wimbledon. The latter victory came at the expense of Margaret Smith Court. Newcomers just didn't beat the formidable, highly experienced Court. But this newcomer did: not only at Wimbledon but also earlier, in the Tasmanian championships. (Court gained revenge in the Australian, defeating Goolagong in their two finals.)

Walter Bingham, in *Sports Illustrated*, wrote of Goolagong's 6–4, 6–1 win over Court at Wimbledon: "[Goolagong] destroyed the defending champion. . . . Margaret would move in, crack a deep return, and move confidently to the net, a winning position. But then Evonne would rifle a cross-court backhand, or forehand, an inch over the net and maybe an inch inside the line. Over and over again. She gave a vivid demonstration of how wide and how long a tennis court can be. . . ." Chances are the passing-shot winners were mostly backhands: Goolagong's low backhand slice was a formidable weapon.

Evonne and Margaret shared more than a memorable rivalry. Both bore children while playing professionally, and after a suitable interval, both successfully resumed their careers. Goolagong's '80 Wimbledon victory marked the first time in 66 years that a mother had taken the singles title.

Goolagong's ledger included four consecutive Australian singles titles, two Wimbledons, and a French Open. In her final-round defeats at Forest Hills (1973 to '76), she took the victor to three sets in all but one, a 6–3, 6–0 clobbering by Chris Evert. In two of those extended matches, however, she managed only two games in the final set, an indication, perhaps, that graceful movement may come at the expense of strength and staying power.

> **"Winning never consumed Evonne Goolagong. She played tennis as though simply being on the court was the greatest joy in the world."** –Billie Jean King

If four straight huge disappointments upset Goolagong, no one but close friends knew. As always, she remained cheerful and charming. Nor did fans desert her. Whatever the end result, they considered it a treat to see her get there. Winning or losing, Goolagong looked better than anyone else: lithe and fluid in every movement and every stroke, so smooth she made others look jerky. She was more than poetry in motion; she was music in motion, modern dance with a racquet, in short, the way we'd all like to look on a court when people are watching.

As Billie Jean King, who had her share of tough matches against Goolagong, reflected in her history of the women's game, "Winning never consumed Evonne Goolagong. She played tennis as though simply being on the court was the greatest joy in the world."

U.S. Open resume: Finalist in 1973, '74, '75, and '76.

THE LEGENDS
Billie Jean King

Unlike anyone before or after her, Billie Jean King has had two distinct tennis careers: oncourt, one of the toughest and most successful competitors ever; offcourt, a tireless and effective crusader for women's rights. As future histories are written, her name will loom larger and larger, eventually overshadowing even her own performance as a player.

To this day, there is only one "Billie Jean" (no last name necessary): bouncy, feisty, opinionated, above all purposeful.

Early on, she was not only bouncy but also bubbly, a chunky, chubby-cheeked lass. Part of a remarkable family generation (her brother, Randy Moffitt, pitched in the major leagues), her own background exemplified the democracy that characterized the great era of Southern California tennis. Her father was a Long Beach fireman. Socially, that would have foreclosed many Eastern courts to her, but in California, it was no hindrance at all.

Hers was a hometown-girl-makes-good story of the kind that warms American hearts: touch football as a tomboy; tennis dresses sewn by mother—to whom she declared she'd be No. 1 in the world; coins saved in a Mason jar to pay for her first racquet (violet-colored, $8).

King quit college in her junior year and, with the support of Australian businessman Robert Mitchell (who also sent Margaret Smith Court to charm school), headed Down Under to study with player/coach Mervyn Rose. "He made radical alterations in my game, changing my swooping, wristy forehand and backhand into the crisp, efficient strokes of a champion," she said.

Although barely over 5' 4", she blended those strokes into an attacking style, "which made me one of the smallest net-rushing champions in history." She could win from the backcourt—several clay-court titles, including the French Open singles, proved that—but instinct and knowledge of her own abilities drew her "in." Back or in, she was tenacious, resilient, and terrific in big matches.

One could fill this entire space with King's major titles. They number 39 in all, placing King third on the all-time list (behind Court and Martina Navratilova). King won more U.S. tour titles—whatever the surface—than anyone since the distant Hazel Hotchkiss Wightman. She gathered titles the tennis world over—in many countries, on all surfaces. The majors included six Wimbledons, one Australian, and a French, plus four Forest Hills's; assorted indoors, hard courts, clay courts, etc. She played on 19 Federation Cup and Wightman Cup teams combined.

King was a great doubles player, rivaling Court, Navratilova, and Margaret Osborne duPont as the best ever among females. Prime evidence: her successes with a variety of partners. Her favorite

> ## "To this day, there is only one 'Billie Jean' (no last name necessary): bouncy, feisty, opinionated, above all purposeful."

among them was the short, combative Rosie Casals. Together they won seven majors and became the only women's team to capture U.S. titles on all three surfaces. Pioneers as well as partners, King and Casals were the first top-flight women to use the revolutionary Wilson T2000 racquet.

King was as combative offcourt as on—and a lot more idealistic. As the sport entered the open era, she undertook two crusades: for new rules, tournaments, and circuits; and for equal prize money for women. Logic and gender equity, rather than personal gain, were her principal motivations.

Later, she would be a driving force behind World TeamTennis and the female who put pesky Bobby Riggs in his place. Of the ballyhooed Riggs match, she wrote accurately, "I had shown . . . that women were skillful, entertaining, and capable of coming through in the clutch."

U.S. Open resume: Winner in 1967, '71, '72, '74. Finalist in 1968. Also won five women's and four mixed doubles titles.

THE LEGENDS
Rod Laver

"The Rocket," another bona fide candidate for best-ever, bracketed the end of the amateur era and beginning of the open, with Grand Slams fore and aft. In 1962 as an amateur, and seven years later as a professional, Rod Laver won all four major singles titles. No man before him save Don Budge had won even one Grand Slam; none has done it since. Like Joe DiMaggio's 56-game hitting streak, the double Slam is an achievement likely to withstand modern assaults.

Laver was a physical phenomenon. A son of the Australian bush, he grew up scrawny and in ill health. His career-long nickname was sarcastically applied by his coach, Harry Hopman, who said he

> **"Laver could simply overwhelm an opponent with a barrage of crushing shots launched from anywhere on the court. At the top of his game, he was tennis's all-time whirling dervish."**

was "anything but a rocket." Laver nonetheless developed a super-charged game driven by a lightweight body that, as Bud Collins has written, "seemed to dangle from a massive left arm that belonged to a gorilla."

The Arm produced an arsenal of powerful shots. Topspin drives off both sides were foremost among them. Unlike the legion of backcourters who followed him, Laver was no looping, just-keep-the-ball-in-play topspinner. He took full windups and belted everything that came his way, going for winners, not rallies. (In a Forest Hills semifinal, he almost knocked Rafael Osuna down on four consecutive backhand service returns.)

So wristy were those strokes that somebody once described the backhand version as resembling "a guy flinging rice at newlyweds."

Laver had a lot more than topspin. His slice backhand, unusually hard-hit and forceful, made a terrific approach shot, especially on grass, where it bit into the turf and coaxed a weak return that Laver put away at net. In addition, he was exceedingly quick and agile. On the faster surfaces, his attacking instincts propelled him out of the backcourt and up to net, where he volleyed and hit overheads with the best of his peers.

Laver could simply overwhelm an opponent with a barrage of crushing shots launched from just about anywhere on the court. At the top of his game, he was tennis's all-time whirling dervish.

That same talent made him vulnerable to sloppy errors and upsets, and he lost his share of big matches to some of his principal rivals. For example, he dropped consecutive finals to Neale Fraser and Roy Emerson before winning his first Forest Hills title in 1962, and his first two Wimbledon finals before crushing Chuck McKinley in 1961.

Laver had an unusually concentrated record of success in the major tournaments. Of his 11 singles titles, eight were earned in the Grand Slam years. What years they were. In 1962, he ran off with, besides the four majors, a dizzying string of national championships: the Italian, German, Norwegian, Irish, and Swiss, winning in all 134 of an exhausting 149 matches. His road to victory in the French required overcoming a match point in the quarters and coming through five-setters in both the semis and the final.

Over the next 14 years he won five U.S. Pro Championships in six years; a fifth Davis Cup, this one in 1973, ending a five-year U.S. string; and Rookie of the Year (at age 38) in the World Team Tennis league.

Seven years can be a career, or longer, for ordinary pros. For Laver, that span produced a rebirth of tennis supremacy. In 1969, with his feat of '62 a dimming memory, he fashioned a second Grand Slam, surviving near-elimination by several opponents in the new open era of "contract" and "independent" pros.

Two years later, he became the first tennis player to earn $1 million on the court.

U.S. Open resume: Winner in 1962 and '69. Finalist in men's doubles three times.

THE LEGENDS
Ilie Nastase

It's difficult to imagine a tennis player as simultaneously attractive and repellent as was Ilie Nastase in his prime. Nobody of his era was more gifted, more graceful, more enjoyable to watch as both athlete and shotmaker. And very few behaved worse on the court; against Jimmy Connors, who was close in that respect, Nastase played matches in which the invective was at least as electrifying as the game.

In a sense, Nastase was what open, highly commercialized tennis needed, or at least what it welcomed. He was at times less a player than a Personality, with a string of fines and reprimands—as well as the nickname "Nasty"—to prove it. His extraneous actions helped broaden the sport's appeal, which most people reckon to be a good thing.

As a brash modern celebrity, Nastase, like Connors, personified the Open as it would evolve at Flushing Meadows. Oddly, considering his talents, Nastase won only one singles title there, but it was earned in a stirring final, a come-from-behind, five-set victory over Arthur Ashe. Losing 2–4 in the fourth set and down a break to start the fifth, Nastase reversed the momentum both times. In addition, he was a very impressive four-time winner of the season-ending Masters tournament.

Astute observers fault Nastase less for behavior than failure to develop his tremendous natural abilities. His record in major tournaments supports that claim: only two singles titles (a French Open in addition to the U.S.) and two runner-up finishes at Wimbledon. Some say he lacked respect for himself; that hard-to-prove fault aside, he certainly lacked concentration and tactical self-discipline. From Nastase, any shot—brilliant or bungled—might be forthcoming at any time.

Fred Perry, Britain's all-time great, told a wonderful story about the man's mindset. Nastase was something of a Perry protégé, and at the 1972 Wimbledon, which Perry worked as a TV commentator, the two agreed that Nastase would frequently glance up at the booth to receive prearranged signals—including such injunctions as "cut out the showboating." The arrangement covered all 14 days of Wimbledon.

With the signaling system working smoothly, Nastase made it to the final in fine style. Rain forced postponement of the match until the next day. Nastase proceeded to play without once looking up at Perry—and lost to Stan Smith in five sets. In the locker room, he denounced Perry for double-crossing him. What the hell did that mean? Perry demanded. Replied Nastase, "You made a deal with me for 14 days, but you didn't say anything about the 15th!"

Nastase had what's now called attitude, and he came by it honestly. Growing up in Romania, he played less because he enjoyed tennis than because

> ## "Nobody of his era was more gifted, more graceful, more enjoyable to watch as both athlete and shotmaker. And very few behaved worse on the court."

he enjoyed being an entertainer. As a pro, he reveled in what he called "the element of surprise"—for opponents and fans alike. "I want to attack the rules of tennis," he told *Sports Illustrated*, "and protect myself against rules at the same time." A philosophy like that sanctions all sorts of behavior, and Nastase practiced all sorts, even sitting on the court to pout.

Ironically, he was not the worst Romanian involved in the infamously rowdy 1972 Davis Cup final against the U.S. That dishonor belonged to any number of Bucharest spectators and especially to Nastase's doubles partner, Ion Tiriac. Nasty pretty much just played—and lost.

Nastase in later tennis life has managed to polish his tarnished image. In senior events he has toned down his obnoxious behavior and emphasized his talent for clever shots and even more clever remarks. The result: Nasty has become Ilie the Lovable, a more-or-less harmless bit of alchemy.

U.S. Open resume: Winner in 1972.

John Newcombe

He had the appearance of a benign, good-looking Ion Tiriac: long face, droopy mustache, shaggy hair. The resemblance ended there. Tiriac, the player turned promoter, was a dour, almost menacing Romanian who won two ordinary pro tournaments. John Newcombe was a cheerful, engaging Aussie who won 25 major titles—seven in singles, 18 in doubles.

Then as now, he was known the tennis world over as "Newk." The nickname, with its intimations of good-ole-boy camaraderie, fits neatly. He had an easy grin and All-Australia capacity for swilling beer. (Among tennis players, the competition in that category was fierce.) Dick Stockton captured Newk's beery side in five words: "a 30-year-old boy."

All things considered, however, Newcombe was probably the most mature and nuanced of the great Aussies. He genuinely enjoyed spending time with his family, disliked the grind of the tour, and invested wisely, pouring his earnings into an impressive and popular tennis "ranch" west of San Antonio. (For a fancy fee, several dozen hackers go there each fall to play and party with Newk and several other "Legends" of the game.)

Oncourt, he was the last champion of the Harry Hopman dynasty, which began at mid-century with Frank Sedgman and Ken McGregor and continued through Hoad and Rosewall, Fraser and Emerson, Laver and Stolle, and finally Newcombe and Tony Roche. Newk and "Roachie," a cagey lefthander, formed a doubles team that captured three straight Wimbledon titles and five overall; Newcombe also won Grand Slam doubles events with five other partners.

Like Laver, Newcombe won his two U.S. singles championships several years apart—the first as an amateur, the second as a pro. In 1967, he beat Clark Graebner in three close sets; in 1973, he defeated Jan Kodes, a tenacious clay-courter who surprised everybody on grass, in five.

Newk's game was to pressure the other guy incessantly. He chose the most direct way of doing that, by serving and volleying. By the standards of the '70s, he wielded a big serve, which he accompanied with a big grunt. His second serve was also a weapon. He disdained a defensive, high-bouncing twist, opting instead for a hard slice. It was risky, but it worked. Opponents rarely went for winners or "chipped and charged" against a Newcombe second serve. Instead, they tried simply to keep the return low and prayed for an errant or weak volley.

When Jack Kramer rated the best strokes he'd seen during several decades, Newcombe remarkably finished at or near the top in three categories: best second serve, "by far"; one of the best forehand volleys and overheads. Newk was so confident of

> ## "When Jack Kramer rated the best strokes he'd seen during several decades, Newcombe finished at or near the top in three categories: best second serve, 'by far....' "

crunching or at least retrieving any lob that he crowded in on the net—a perfect position for angling winning volleys. Although Kramer didn't mention it, Newcombe also had a first-class forehand.

Among the top Aussies, many of whom came from rural, working-class backgrounds, Newcombe represented the middle class. His father practiced dentistry in Sydney, and young John swatted tennis balls in the street outside the house. He excelled at other sports, however, and it took him a while to get serious about tennis. His first prime-time exposure came at the age of 19, when he was thrust into a Davis Cup singles spot against the United States. He lost both of his matches, to Dennis Ralston and Chuck McKinley. But those losses were just the opening act in Newcombe's long career. Before he was through, Newk had carried off almost three times as many major titles as Ralston and McKinley combined.

U.S. Open resume: Winner in 1967 and '73. Finalist in 1966. Also won three men's and one mixed doubles titles.

THE LEGENDS
Ken Rosewall

John Newcombe's Fantasy Tennis Camp, 1993, with pros drilling campers: Ken Rosewall runs for every camper shot, even the shanked mis-hits; when the whistle blows to end the session, he lingers oncourt, urging his group to "have just a few more hits." Finally, he scurries around picking up stray balls.

That's Rosewall now, and it was Rosewall then: "Muscles," the living work ethic. At a slender 5'7", he was smaller even than Rod Laver. But unlike Laver, Rosewall never tried to exceed the logical limitations of his size. He guided rather than blasted his ground strokes and—unless fast courts dictated otherwise—merely placed his first serve.

In fact, Rosewall couldn't have blasted his auntie off the court. He sliced, diced, and delicately skewered his opponents, not with soft stuff but with surgical precision. Most of all, he anticipated shots beautifully. Preparation is one key to playing good tennis, and Rosewall was Mr. Preparation.

Among the stroke-conscious, however, he is remembered for his backhand—the best ever excepting, perhaps, Don Budge. Rosewall's version was a model of economy: short backswing and stroke, enough underspin to control the ball perfectly. (When somebody told me, years ago, "You have a backhand like Rosewall's"—i.e., it looks like Rosewall's—I considered that the greatest tennis compliment I ever received.)

But Rosewall was an all-court player, which he proved after Pancho Gonzales beat him conclusively in the first year of their pro tour. Rosewall promptly changed to Gonzales's game—the indoor game—and served and volleyed so effectively thereafter that he held his own against Gonzales and succeeded him as world professional champion.

In the mind of the true fan, Rosewall will be forever twinned with Lew Hoad. Born 21 days apart in the same city, Sydney, they went through the juniors, the Australian national tournaments, and onto the overseas tour in virtual lockstep.

As 17-year-olds in 1952, both reached the quar-terfinals at Forest Hills, with Rosewall ousting the U.S. No. 1, Vic Seixas. For the next several years, Rosewall and Hoad leapfrogged each other in tournament play. Their most memorable head-to-head year was 1956, when Hoad beat Rosewall in the Australian and Wimbledon finals; Rosewall, two months later, reversed the result at Forest Hills. The loss cost Hoad the Grand Slam.

In the early 1980s, when I asked Hoad to compare his results with Rosewall's, I expected him to shelter behind the back problem that cut short his own illustrious career. Instead, he cited Rosewall's matchless work ethic: "The back wasn't the real difference. I was lazy, while Kenny was very disciplined

> ## "He sliced, diced, and delicately skewered his opponents, not with soft stuff but with surgical precision. Most of all, he anticipated shots beautifully."

and serious." Rosewall, his old friend and nemesis made clear, deserved every bit of his success.

Later on, Rosewall developed another memorable rivalry—with Laver. Although most observers place "Rocket" above "Muscles" in the tennis firmament, the latter held up his end of the pairing. They split their two meetings in Grand Slam finals; in the World Championship Tennis finals in 1971 and '72, Rosewall won on both occasions, the second a 3½-hour battle that gave the sport a big boost with the TV-watching public.

Decades hence, Rosewall's longevity will be best remembered—especially at the U.S. Open. There, at the age of 35, he captured his second singles title, 14 years after the first. At 39, he beat John Newcombe and continued on to the finals. Never mind that Jimmy Connors crushed him on that occasion; to many people, non-fans as well as fans, the still-trim and sinewy "Muscles" had won the day.

U.S. Open resume: Winner in 1956 and '70. Finalist in 1955 and '74. Also won two men's doubles titles.

THE LEGENDS
Stan Smith

In the early '70s, when some tennis players were becoming unpleasant personalities, everybody liked Stan Smith. He was intelligent, gracious, sincere, and best of all, in an era of rising voice levels, soft-spoken. He was also a pleasure to watch: 6' 4", slim, blond, and handsome, with a big game that had deftness as well as plenty of power.

The power was inherent, the deftness acquired. As *The New York Times*'s Neil Amdur related, Smith, as a high school boy, "offered his services as a ballboy for a Davis Cup match but was turned down because officials thought he was too clumsy to run across the court and pick up balls." From that ignominious start came one of the finest Davis Cup players ever to represent any nation: During a highly successful period for U.S. teams, Smith won 22 of 24 Cup matches, and in all but six of them, he clinched the U.S. victory.

Smith grew up in Pasadena and was named All-America at USC. His doubles partner there was Bob Lutz. They went on to become the best U.S. doubles team of their era, Davis Cup stalwarts, and four-time winners of the U.S. Open. (Smith virtually owned Lutz in singles—though many of the matches were close—but that seemed not to diminish their friendship.)

Smith's career was oddly top-heavy with Davis Cup laurels. He won only two majors in singles—the Open in 1971, Wimbledon the following year. But the Wimbledon victory, a five-setter over Ilie Nastase, makes most of the best-ever lists for that tournament. The Open title came at the expense of Jan Kodes, a clay-courter who had managed to adapt his game to grass. That was only the second year of the tiebreak system, and Smith used a tiebreak to polish off Kodes in their fourth set. Much earlier, however, he had decided the outcome by changing tactics: Seeing Kodes handle his flat serve effectively, Smith switched to a spin delivery at the start of the second set and took command of the match.

For drama and significance, none of Smith's tournament victories was more noteworthy than his performance in the 1972 Davis Cup final against Romania. Considering the adverse conditions, it was plain heroic. The U.S. team, with Smith winning both of his singles, had beaten Romania's Nastase and Ion Tiriac the previous year in Charlotte, North Carolina. Now the competition would be in Bucharest, and the Romanians were primed for an upset. They needed help from the home crowd and the judges who were, shall we say, patriotic. They got both, so the decision rode on whether the Americans, superior in skill, could withstand the extracurricular assaults and pull out a victory.

> ## "Everybody liked Stan Smith. He was intelligent, gracious, sincere, and best of all, in an era of rising voice levels, soft-spoken. He was also a pleasure to watch...."

Smith's singles cohort, Tom Gorman, could not. After winning the first two sets against Tiriac, he lost the match as his opponent complained repeatedly about line calls and orchestrated a growing anti-American crowd response. Smith had defeated Nastase without serious incident, so the team match stood at 1–1. Smith and Erik van Dillen won the doubles easily the next day. With Gorman still shaken from his first-match experience, the outcome would in all probability hinge on Smith's ability to beat Tiriac.

Beat him Smith did, despite bad line calls, crowd heckling, and oncourt antics that made Tiriac's earlier behavior seem trivial. When the match came down to the fifth set, Smith raised his game a full level and won it at love. Then he said, "Ion, I must tell you that I will always respect you as a player. But I will never again respect you as a man." Set, match, and conversational slam—Stan Smith.

U.S. Open resume: Winner in 1971.

THIRD SET: THE

MOVE TO FLUSHING 1978–1987

THIRD SET
The Move to Flushing
1978–1987

New stadium, new surface—new game? Not really. Only two of the players who won U.S. Open singles titles after the event migrated crosstown—John McEnroe and Boris Becker—could not logically have won them on the old Har-Tru surface at Forest Hills. One other, Pete Sampras, might have had difficulty. Neither McEnroe nor Becker, aggressive players who depend on serve-and-volley, have done well on "clay"; Becker, in fact, has never won a clay event throughout his entire career, although both deserve credit for having continued to try. Sampras has captured a couple of clay titles, but not yet—at least through 1996—a major one.

The other winners at Flushing Meadows have been successful on both hard and soft surfaces. Jimmy Connors and Chris Evert won at both U.S. Open venues. And it's probable that only the accident of birth dates kept Steffi Graf, Monica Seles, Ivan Lendl, Martina Navratilova, and maybe a couple of others from performing the same feat.

What the move to Flushing has done is to require players to possess a variety of skills. Strictly backcourt players, unless they possess the skill of Bjorn Borg or the lashing ground strokes of Lendl or Thomas Muster, cannot even hope to win men's events on the DecoTurf II at Flushing. And since Evert's time, one-dimensional backcourters have had less influence there. Again there's an exception: Seles, who has, or had, Lendl's ability to pulverize the ball from the baseline. In any case, the average American fan likes the change. If he wants endless top-spin rallies, he can fall asleep watching the French Open on TV.

Perhaps this stems from nostalgia blindness, but the first decade at Flushing seems to have been exceptionally rich in personalities, drama, and great days at

The move to a new stadium (right) produces some stunning new views as well as some new stars, including Tracy Austin (left), who defeats Chris Evert in 1979 for her first Open singles title.

McEnroe (far right) wins his second consecutive Open in 1980 with a "gut-wrenching" win over Borg, 7–6, 6–1, 6–7, 5–7, 6–4. Has there ever been a more captivating high-wire act than McEnroe?

the tournament. By my reckoning, any rundown of those categories would include the following entries:

• McEnroe's tenacious, gut-wrenching, five-set victory over Borg in the 1980 singles final; and McEnroe's tumultuous night match with Ilie Nastase—a Nastase in full theatrical flower—a year earlier.

• Connors's purported greatest shot in Open history, a backhand hit around the net post for a down-the-line winner in the decisive game against Adriano Panatta in 1978.

• Lendl's three straight titles in the mid-'80s, following hard on his three straight runner-up finishes and emphatically rebutting the charge that he couldn't win the big ones.

• The repeated and still somewhat inexplicable failures of Borg, the backcourter who conquered fast grass at Wimbledon but could not do the same on the medium-speed hard courts at Flushing Meadows.

• The swift, endearing rise and tragic fall of Tracy Austin.

• The last great years of Evert, foreshadowed by the loss of the 1979 final to Austin.

• Lori McNeil's flash of fame in 1987, when she ousted Evert and gave Graf a scare; the ascendance of McNeil and the more enduring Zina Garrison, pals from the Houston ghetto, as the first black women to challenge for a major title since the days of Althea Gibson.

• Navratilova's stunning match-point double fault to lose her first Open final in 1981.

• Pam Shriver's victory in '82 over Navratilova, her doubles partner and singles nemesis-for-life, an event that reduced the loser to public tears; Navratilova's strong rebound the following year, capped by a smashing 6–1, 6–3 win over Evert in the final.

• Was half of this "set" played in 1979, or does it just seem that way? What a year at the Open! Not so much for great tennis as for memorable, and often quirky, events. Almost no one was accustomed to night matches, the roar of engines overhead, and the bustle and inopportune shouts of the crowds. But none of that could have accounted for a serve by Roscoe Tanner breaking the net.

All the pizzazz could, however, help account for

CLASSIC MATCHES

1986 SEMIFINAL:
MARTINA NAVRATILOVA VERSUS STEFFI GRAF

It signaled the onset—but not the culmination—of generational change in the women's game: Navratilova, almost 30 years old and 12 years into her professional career, was on the down slope; Graf, 17, with strong legs and the biggest female forehand around, was just gathering momentum. A photo of the two coming off the court captures the significance: the woman looking ruefully, wistfully, at the girl—whom she's just beaten. Rain halted play and forced an overnight postponement with Navratilova ahead 4–1 in the first set; next day, she ran it out, 6–1. Back came Graf, riding that forehand, blasting an astonishing 27 ground-stroke winners en route to winning a tiebreak. Navratilova resurgent: up 4–2 in the third set, with a break point for 5–2. The unruly teenager subdued? Hardly. She held in that game and also won the next two. At 4–5, Graf had a pair of match points. Navratilova saved both, one with the gutsy move of a seasoned campaigner: She came to net behind her second serve and her surprised opponent dumped a routine backhand into the net. Several minutes later, tiebreak time arrived again. Now it was Graf saving match points, two of them. She parlayed the second into an 8–7 lead: yet another match point, with Navratilova serving. The veteran had one spurt of pressure tennis left, and she used it. She coaxed a netted passing shot, punched a good volley to force an error, and, finally, hit a heavy, spinning serve to the backhand that Graf could only net.

1980 FINAL:
BJORN BORG VERSUS JOHN MCENROE

Borg and McEnroe came to this match with memories of the titanic, 34-point tiebreak they had played earlier in the summer at Wimbledon. And Borg came to it with something more: a declared goal, unusual for him, of winning this tournament—for the very first time. Both men had played long matches earlier in the week; McEnroe had survived a five-setter with Jimmy Connors less than 24 hours before the final began. Nonetheless, he took the first two sets, reeling off 13 straight points in the second. Borg, grooving his backhand passing shots, recovered to win the next two. Having won 13 five-setters without a loss since 1976, Borg seemed to be in command. But the fifth here was played under lights, which often seemed to bother Borg. Sensing that, McEnroe cranked up his first-serve percentage to an impressive 70 and knocked off a flock of first volleys. He got the one service break he needed and ran out the set, and match, 6–4. "I thought," said the weary victor, "my body was going to fall off."

the zany doings when Nastase met McEnroe. The early-round match bore some resemblance to tag-team wrestling or St. Patrick's Day in New York City. It featured cups thrown oncourt by spectators in their cups, a running exchange of insults between Nasty and veteran umpire Frank Hammond, the latter's default of the former, and tournament director Bill Talbert's reversal of the default. When McEnroe, who behaved relatively well, went on to win the wretched affair, the result was anticlimactic.

The rest of the tournament also had its oddities. Four American men reached the semis of "their" tournament, and the two who survived—McEnroe and Vitas Gerulaitis—could have walked to the final from their boyhood homes in Queens. As the well-rested beneficiary of a second default, by the injured Eddie Dibbs in the quarters, Mac won this neighborhood scrimmage handily. The women's event was far more dignified, and it made conventional history: Austin, at 16 years, nine months of age, became the youngest U.S. champion.

"I thought the title might intimidate her," said Evert, the loser, who saw her 34-match Open winning streak brought to an end. "But she was out there like it was just another tennis match." With a big-sisterly pat on the shoulder from Evert, Austin left the court grinning like a schoolgirl who had just landed a prom date with the class heartthrob.

A year later, Austin felt the first stabbing pains of sciatica.

They signaled the beginning of her losing battle with injuries, a battle that drove her from the game, as a frequent and star performer, before her 21st birthday. Other young women, notably Andrea Jaeger and Hungary's Andrea Temesvari, have suffered similar injury-plagued careers. Billie Jean King later wrote of the "ominous trend. The unrelenting intensity of the professional circuit would take a toll on the young and still-growing competitors . . . the child stars of the late 1970s and early 1980s. . . ."

Older and endowed with bodies that stood up better to the incessant pounding, the men were suffering few physical breakdowns. In 1985, after being thrashed in two finals by Connors and one by

Garrison (below, left) and McNeil become the first black women to contend for a major since Gibson; friends and frequent doubles partners, Shriver (below, right) and Navratilova walk off the court after Shriver's surprising upset of Navratilova in the 1982 quarterfinals.

McEnroe, Czech-born Ivan Lendl brought his Americanization to its tennis climax. He reversed the '84 result by beating McEnroe in straight sets, then took the next two titles over countryman Miloslav Mecir (about whom Lendl made a famous prefinal comment that he would rather be fishing) and Mats Wilander. The impressive three-peat gained Lendl respect but not affection. His coolly smashing girl friend, Samantha Frankel, seemed to be the only one ready to give him that.

Wilander, a soft-spoken, amiable man, engineered his own rebound and beat Lendl for the championship in 1988. The match didn't enthrall too many spectators: at least one-quarter of them had bailed out by the start of the fifth set. It did make the state of Connecticut proud. Both these finalists, one by way of Czechoslovakia, the other Sweden, were now neighbors in the posh town of Greenwich. Shades of Mac and Vitas circa '79, but with more trees and a nice zoning code.

The Era in Pictures 1978–1987

Sixteen-year-old Pam Shriver (above) plays her way into the singles final to become the latest ingenue to charm the Open crowds, this time at the tournament's new home in Flushing Meadows. Unfortunately for Shriver, she runs into another former prodigy by the name of Chris Evert, who summarily dispatches her, 7–5, 6–4, in the championship match. It is the fourth straight singles title for Evert, who can then sit back and enjoy the men's final, in which her former Jimmy Connors (right) defeats Bjorn Borg in straight sets to become the first man to win the Open on three different surfaces—grass, clay and the hard courts of the new tennis center in Flushing.

1978

CHAMPIONS

SINGLES
Jimmy Connors
Chris Evert

DOUBLES
Bob Lutz
& Stan Smith

Billie Jean King
& Martina Navratilova

MIXED DOUBLES
Betty Stove
& Frew McMillan

"Jimmy [Connors] was born on this stuff. This is his court. I saw he was on top of his game from the beginning. There was not much I could do."

—Bjorn Borg

"They hate us. Popularity-wise, I'm a notch above John [McEnroe], and John is a notch above Son of Sam."

—Vitas Gerulaitis

1979

CHAMPIONS

SINGLES
John McEnroe
Tracy Austin

DOUBLES
John McEnroe
& Peter Fleming

Betty Stove
& Wendy Turnbull

MIXED DOUBLES
Greer Stevens
& Bob Hewitt

The youth movement in tennis continues as 16-year-old Tracy Austin becomes the youngest champion in U.S. Open history. En route to the title, she defeats No. 2 seed Martina Navratilova in the semifinals and reigning champ Chris Evert Lloyd in the final. In the men's draw, the crowds hoot and jeer the two brash local boys from Long Island in the final, Vitas Gerulaitis (right) and John McEnroe. McEnroe emerges victorious with the first of his three U.S. Open titles; for Gerulaitis, it will be his only trip to the Flushing final.

1980

CHAMPIONS

SINGLES
John McEnroe
Chris Evert Lloyd

DOUBLES
Bob Lutz
& Stan Smith

Billie Jean King
& Martina Navratilova

MIXED DOUBLES
Wendy Turnbull
& Marty Riessen

"Andrea will be better than—I don't want to tell Chrissie or Tracy this—but she will be great player."

–Hana Mandlikova
on Andrea Jaeger

Andrea Jaeger (left), just 15 and replete with braces and pigtails, becomes the youngest player to make it to an Open semifinal, where she loses to Hana Mandlikova. Mandlikova will fall in the final to Chris Evert Lloyd, who wins her fifth title in six years.

On the men's side, John McEnroe (right), he of the feathery touch and uncanny anticipation, wins his second straight, defeating Bjorn Borg in an unforgettable five-set final, 7–6, 6–1, 6–7, 5–7, 6–4.

1981

CHAMPIONS

SINGLES
John McEnroe
Tracy Austin

DOUBLES
John McEnroe
& Peter Fleming

Anne Smith
& Kathy Jordan

MIXED DOUBLES
Anne Smith
& Kevin Curren

*Tracy Austin (right)
wins her second Open
title, defeating Martina
Navratilova, who is
making her first finals
appearance and who
double-faults on match
point in a close match
that goes in Austin's
favor, 1–6, 7–6, 7–6.
Navratilova will be back.
Bjorn Borg (left) appears
in the final for the fourth
and last time and fails
again, losing to
John McEnroe, who
becomes the first man
since Bill Tilden in the
'20s to win three straight
U.S. singles titles. Borg
will never appear in a
Grand Slam final again
and his futility in the
U.S. Open remains the
only blemish on his
sterling career.*

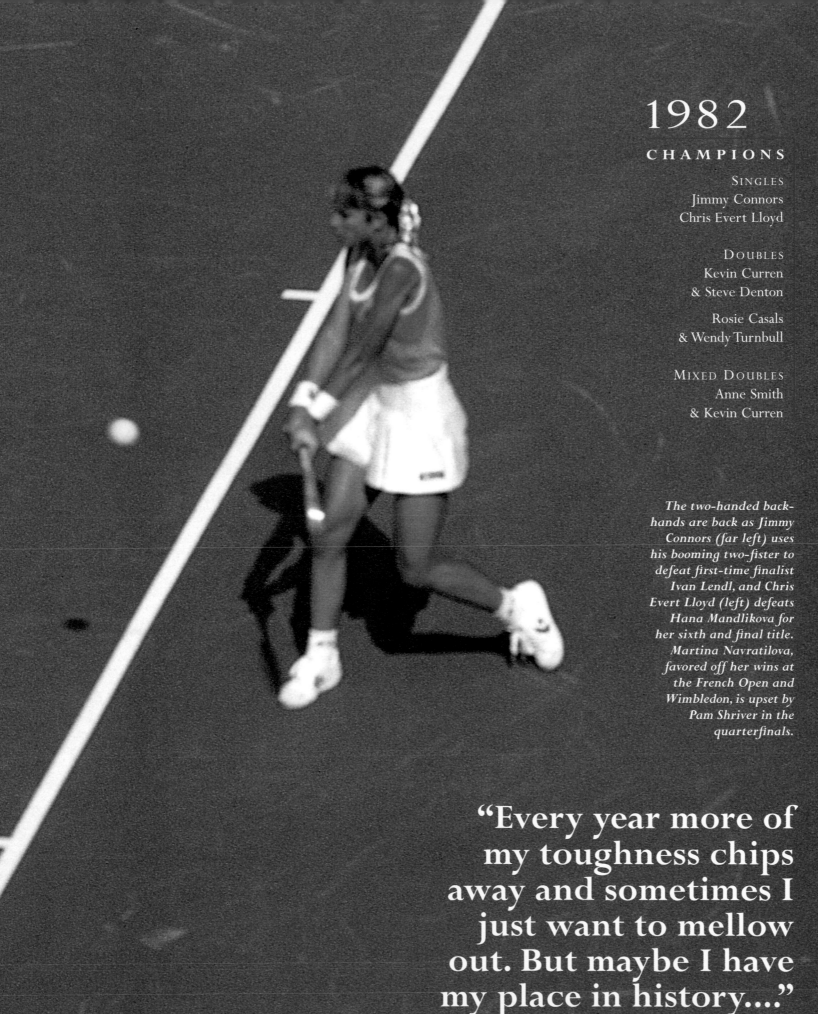

1982

CHAMPIONS

SINGLES
Jimmy Connors
Chris Evert Lloyd

DOUBLES
Kevin Curren
& Steve Denton

Rosie Casals
& Wendy Turnbull

MIXED DOUBLES
Anne Smith
& Kevin Curren

The two-handed back-hands are back as Jimmy Connors (far left) uses his booming two-fister to defeat first-time finalist Ivan Lendl, and Chris Evert Lloyd (left) defeats Hana Mandlikova for her sixth and final title. Martina Navratilova, favored off her wins at the French Open and Wimbledon, is upset by Pam Shriver in the quarterfinals.

"Every year more of my toughness chips away and sometimes I just want to mellow out. But maybe I have my place in history...."
–Chris Evert

"You win one big match and that's enough of a taste of winning to keep you going. But there's an arrogance you must have, and only two of them have that."

—Pam Shriver on Chris Evert and Martina Navratilova

1983

The torch is passed: After struggling mightily in her previous Open efforts, Martina Navratilova (above, right) finally brings her 'A' game to Flushing, breezing past Chris Evert *Lloyd, 6–1, 6–3, in the final. Jimmy Connors defeats Ivan Lendl for the men's title, while John McEnroe (far right) and Peter Fleming win their third doubles title in five years.*

1984

"New Yorkers love it when you spill your guts out there. You spill your guts at Wimbledon, they make you stop and clean it up."

–Jimmy Connors before his gritty semifinal loss to John McEnroe

Mac is back: John McEnroe (left) survives a dramatic five-set semifinal with Jimmy Connors, then goes on to defeat Ivan Lendl in straight sets for his fourth and final U.S. Open title. Martina Navratilova defeats Chris Evert Lloyd in the final for the second straight year, though this time the score is much closer—4–6, 6–4, 6–4. Navratilova teams with Pam Shriver (above, left) to win the women's doubles title as well. It is the second straight doubles championship for the peerless pair, who will win two more over the next three years.

1985

CHAMPIONS

SINGLES
Ivan Lendl
Hana Mandlikova

DOUBLES
Ken Flach
& Robert Seguso

Claudia Kohde-Kilsch
& Helena Sukova

MIXED DOUBLES
Martina Navratilova
& Heinz Gunthardt

Two new champions are crowned in Flushing Meadows: Ivan Lendl (above), after three consecutive losing appearances in the finals, breaks through, defeating defending champion John McEnroe 7–6, 6–3, 6–4 for the first of his three straight titles; and Hana Mandlikova (right), herself the victim of a pair of final-match losses in the past, guts out a dramatic win over Martina Navratilova, 7–6, 1–6, 7–6, for her one and only U.S. Open singles championship.

The hearts of Czechoslovakians are bursting with pride as all four singles finalists were born in that then-intact nation. Miloslav Mecir (left) is defeated by Ivan Lendl for the title, nonetheless achieving the distinction of becoming the lowest seed, at No. 16, to reach the finals since 1971. In the women's final, the un-stoppable Martina Navratilova (below) wins her third title in four years, beating Helena Sukova in straight sets.

1986

CHAMPIONS

SINGLES
Ivan Lendl
Martina Navratilova

DOUBLES
Andres Gomez
& Slobodan Zivojinovic

Pam Shriver
& Martina Navratilova

MIXED DOUBLES
Raffaella Reggi
& Sergio Casal

1987

The more things change…. Again the champions are Ivan Lendl (left), who outlasts Mats Wilander in a four-set marathon that goes nearly five hours, and Martina Navratilova (right), who beats relatively unknown 18-year-old Steffi Graf in straight sets. It is a banner year for Navratilova, who also emerges with titles in women's doubles (with Pam Shriver) and mixed doubles (with Emilio Sánchez).

Tracy Austin

When Tracy Austin won her two singles titles at the U.S. Open, she reacted like the teenager she was. No fist pumping; no kneeling on the court to thank the god of tennis. Austin jumped up and down in girlish delight and flashed the guileless smile of a kid whose biggest Christmas wish had just come true.

Born into an accomplished tennis family in the Los Angeles area, Austin blew like a fresh breeze across the Grand Slam scene. Not that her principal rivals were old or stale. Chris Evert was in mid-career and still America's tennis sweetheart; Martina Navratilova was just beginning to really roll. But Austin was delightfully different. Unlike the reserved, self-controlled Evert and the muscularly athletic Navratilova, she was open, spontaneous, seemingly vulnerable, the proverbial girl-next-door from a more innocent era in American life.

She was also a true tennis prodigy. Before hitting the big time, she had won 22 age-group titles, beginning with the national 12-and-under when she was a mere 10. In her first appearance at Forest Hills in 1977, standing a pigtailed 4' 11" and weighing in at 89 pounds (including the braces on her teeth), she fought her way into the quarterfinals, upending Sue Barker, the fourth seed and a future French Open champion.

By 1979, Austin was up to 5' 4" and 110, and she was no longer sporting the gingham-trimmed pinafores she'd worn two years earlier. More important, whatever ideas opponents had of her as a sweet little girl had evaporated. According to Billie Jean King in *We Have Come a Long Way*, "Chris summed it up by saying, '[Austin] was tough. She had determination and control over situations. I could see it in her eyes.' "

She did beat Evert at Flushing Meadows that year, toppling the four-time national champion by the routine score of 6–4, 6–3. Austin used no magic: She simply beat the champ at her own, methodical baseline game. In the semifinals, she'd won a closer match over Navratilova. At 16 years, nine months, Austin had become the youngest-ever U.S. Nationals titleholder.

Years later, Austin recalled the prologue to that victory over Evert. Driving to Flushing from Long Island with her family, she said, "I was so relaxed. We were joking and laughing in the car, playing some silly word game with tongue twisters. I was laughing hysterically. And then I played Chrissie. I didn't know how important the Open was."

In 1981, the leading ladies of women's tennis were again in the Open spotlight. This time, Navratilova faced Evert in the semis and eked out a three-set victory. Next day, in her first Open final, she raced through Austin, 6–1, in the first set. At that point, Austin subsequently recalled, "I just wanted to try to get some games." She wound up

> **"Austin was open, spontaneous, seemingly vulnerable, the proverbial girl-next-door from a more innocent era in American life."**

getting the next two sets, both in tiebreaks, the kind of pressure situation that has undone many more experienced players. Austin won the third-set breaker with the loss of only one point.

In the period between those two titles, Austin suffered a sudden pain in her buttock. It was diagnosed as sciatica. Eight months of rest and rehabilitation restored her to fighting trim, and she played through the '81 season without major difficulty. But the physical reprieve was only temporary. Early the following year, the pain returned. Austin played on, winning one last title, in San Diego. She tried gamely to return to the tour but couldn't make it. As if the sciatic injury weren't enough, she was also involved in a near-fatal auto accident in 1989.

Without question, Austin is the best player ever to win only three Grand Slam events—the two Open singles and a Wimbledon mixed doubles. Without question, she is also the unluckiest.

U.S. Open resume: Winner in 1979 and '81.

THE LEGENDS
Bjorn Borg

Asked why, in the process of winning six French Opens and five Wimbledons, he was unable to win a single U.S. Open, Bjorn Borg talks about tough competition and says how happy he is to have done as well as he did at Flushing Meadows. It's a stunning answer, or non-answer. Borg vanquished the same competition 11 times in those other two Grand Slams. And how could anyone who had won so often elsewhere be pleased with a U.S. Open record that included four failed trips to the final plus one to the semis and one to the quarters?

Without doubt the prevailing conditions at Flushing Meadows—airplane noise, sometimes-boisterous crowds, night matches for headliners like Borg—played a substantial role. But as one amateur tennis historian points out, anybody who managed to beat adored Italians at the rowdy Italian Open, as the Swede did, can certainly handle distractions. Out of sportsmanship or distaste for controversy, Borg has always kept his real U.S. Open problems locked inside him.

Borg spearheaded a remarkable and in some ways disquieting phenomenon in Swedish tennis. Remarkable in that his success touched off a zeal for the game that carried the small, chilly country to the zenith of international tennis; Edberg, Wilander, Nystrom, Pernfors, and numerous others, the image of Borg firmly in their mind's eye, took to the courts and stayed there, tutored by a unique network of local, essentially amateur coaches. Disquieting in that he launched a trend of quitting school—high school—in favor of professional careers; never mind the fact that few would really make it as pros, and many would be left to cope as latter-day versions of the classic tennis bum.

A very different criticism holds that Borg (in concert with Guillermo Vilas) set in motion a style of play that almost smothered top-level tennis in boredom. Loopy, top-spin shots replaced drives; endless backcourt rallies replaced not only serve-and-volley but also groundstroke-and-volley—and the long-standing tenet that offense was good and necessary. (After the interminable first game of Vilas's 1982 French Open final against Mats Wilander, British journalist Rex Bellamy announced to his colleagues in the press box, "They're playing best of five days.")

Still, it's hard to rate Borg's overall influence on the game as less than positive. It wasn't his fault that others with less talent carried his style to stultifying extremes. He himself was no mere retriever. He could control the play from backcourt, hit terrific passing shots and lobs, and, from mid-career on, serve-and-volley when needed. Borg gave the term pressure player new meaning; nobody was ever

> ## "Borg gave the term pressure player new meaning; nobody was ever more coolly concentrated during stomach-knotting situations...."

more coolly concentrated during stomach-knotting situations, like the famous tiebreak against John McEnroe at Wimbledon in 1980. And for sheer tennis achievements, it's hard to surpass the five consecutive Wimbledon titles he won on the surface serve-and-volleyers love best—a feat akin to light infantry besting heavy armor on a dry plain.

Not so obviously impressive, but rare among today's top pros, was Borg's willingness to work on his game when the stakes were high. Coming up to the '76 Wimbledon, he'd had a sniff of success: two quarterfinal showings in three years. Determined to go beyond that, he spent two pretournament weeks practicing serve-and-volley. The result: his first Wimbledon title, a straight-set thrashing of Ilie Nastase. Four years later, same place, same round, he lost the fourth-set tiebreak to McEnroe, 18–16, failing to convert five match points along the way. Many good players would have wavered, perhaps folded. Instead, Borg went on to win the fifth set—and his fifth title.

U.S. Open resume: Finalist in 1976, '78, '80, and '81.

THE LEGENDS
Jimmy Connors

When 39-year-old Jimmy Connors played and swaggered his way into the semifinals of the 1991 U.S. Open, the achievement represented more than a stagey and improbable climax to his career. It also marked the most impressive demonstration of the qualities whose blending made the career unique: tennis ability and showmanship.

Connors deserves the title "Mr. U.S. Open." Between 1974 and 1983, he won the event five times and was runner-up two others. Between '74 and '78, he gained the finals every year, the first man to threaten Bill Tilden's record. Most notably, Connors won the Open on all three surfaces on which it's been contested: grass and then clay at Forest Hills, hard at Flushing Meadows. And he won it by beating the best players of his time (save John McEnroe) in the finals: Bjorn Borg twice, Ivan Lendl twice.

Those Open victories over Borg and Lendl display Connors's penchant for the big, dramatic moment. Over the course of their respective careers, he trailed both of them, as well as McEnroe, in head-to-head competition. Yet when a "title bout" on his native turf came along, he rose to the occasion.

And when he rose, as he did so often (98 matches won, a record for the tournament), it was not on the strength of his racquet alone. It was also on his ability to generate, and to profit from, the exhilarating emotion of competition. "Jimbo"—the jaunty nickname has stuck to him—set the tone for the modern U.S. championships. Pumping his fist, strutting like a prize cock in the fighting pit, he brought a new level of excitement to the more heterogeneous and democratic crowds—his kinds of crowds—that filled the big stadium at Flushing Meadows. Before pro basketball discovered "showtime," Jimbo introduced it to tennis.

Along with Ilie Nastase, he also introduced temperamental outbursts as a feature of pro matches. On a broader iconoclastic scale, he disdained the Davis Cup, in which he rarely participated, and refused to join the male pros' "union" or to abide by its rules.

Yet true fans will remember, even revere, Jimmy Connors, The Player. Did anyone ever patrol a tennis court with such a compelling combination of skill, zeal, and competitive drive? Watching Connors play with a full head of steam was a primally satisfying experience. In a sense, he was Everyman—in Everyman's dreams—making the utmost of his athletic abilities, fighting to the very end, exulting in victory. The clenched, upraised fist-cum-snarl, which Connors invented and many others have copied, seemed . . . well, ungentlemanly. But it was also deeply satisfying, even to spectators, an assertive, arrogant affirmation of the maxim, "Just Do It!"

Connors was bred to be a tennis champion by his

> ## "He was Everyman—in Everyman's dreams—making the most of his athletic abilities, fighting to the very end, exulting in victory."

mother, Gloria, a local teaching pro in southern Illinois. She helped him develop the two-handed backhand and slashing style of play that would become, respectively, his best shot and his trademark. Saying "his" best shot slights the stroke; it was the best of its kind in tennis history. So, too, some contend, was his service return, which kept the huge servers of the time volleying from their shoe tops or lunging for the sidelines. And like all of the greats, Connors played the big points magnificently.

He has been criticized for failing to develop a more effective first serve and rarely varying his overall game. (Arthur Ashe made him pay for that stubbornness in the famous 1975 Wimbledon final.) But criticizing Connors for sticking with his style of tennis is the ultimate argument with success. If he could sing, at least as well as McEnroe plays guitar, he might warble defiantly, "I did it my-y-y way."

U.S. Open resume: Winner in 1974, '76, '78, '82, and '83. Finalist in 1975 and '77. Also won one men's doubles title.

Chris Evert

In stadiums, on television, and beyond, the public loved her. Pitted against bigger, stronger, more athletic opponents, she vanquished them over and over again. Some people dubbed her the Ice Maiden, and she certainly seemed icily composed in even the most unnerving situations. But that was a slighting phrase that acknowledged only part of Chris Evert's appeal.

More revealing was the widely applied nickname Chrissie, which reflected her basic persona: girlish at the outset of her career, ladylike later on; uncomplaining and gracious in the face of difficulty or defeat. As seen by the public, everything about Evert—her walk and gestures, even the way she ran for the ball—exuded class and femininity. In her late teens, Billie Jean King has noted, Evert made statements like, "No point is worth falling down over."

That was not the real, inner Evert, of course, especially not as she matured into a great champion. At 32 she said, "To be a top tennis player, you have to have a tough streak in you." Both mentally and physically, she was plenty tough. She rarely wilted. She concentrated like a heart surgeon and wasted no time on emotions or other irrelevancies. "Nerves," she said, "don't enter into it at all."

In purely tennis terms, Evert made the absolute most of a limited game. Limited, that is, in what she did well: hit ground strokes. Her serve was mediocre, sometimes weak. Her volley was Grade B; her overhead, sound but not forceful. But she could hit forehands or backhands with any woman who has ever played, and she had a fine, well-disguised drop shot.

Precise, unerring, relentless, she didn't just get the ball back. She also hit winners and shots that set up easy put-aways. Opponents almost had to come to net to beat her, and once there, they faced an array of brilliant passing shots.

Evert learned the game—and gained her strong physical conditioning—on the courts of hot, humid south Florida. Her father, Jimmy, a former top player, taught her everything she knew—including (ironically, in that he never intended her to keep it) the two-handed backhand that became her trademark. Too weak to use one hand as a small girl, she declined to switch later.

Bud Collins has pointed out some of Evert's lesser-known achievements over her 20-year career: a singles won-loss record of 1,309–146 for a winning percentage of .8996, the highest in pro history; at least one major singles title in 13 consecutive years; from 1973–79, 125 consecutive victories on clay; seven titles and 72 victories—both the most ever—at the French Open.

Great rivalries make for great matches, and Evert

> **"She concentrated like a heart surgeon and wasted no time on emotions or other irrelevancies. 'Nerves,' she said, 'don't enter into it.'"**

had both. In the 1970s, the other party was Evonne Goolagong, with Evert holding a decided advantage; in the 1980s, as everyone familiar with professional tennis knows, it was Martina Navratilova. In personality as well as style of play, the two contrasted sharply, and although they became good friends, their head-to-head competition never lost its edge.

The backcourter and frontcourter played twice—1983 and '84—in a U.S. Open final. They were Evert's last appearances in the final, and Navratilova won both times, the first decisively, the second in a very tight three sets. Evert was in the twilight of her career at that point. Back on clay, however, she still had two trumps to play; in 1985 and '86, she defeated Navratilova in three-setters that rank among the best of their 80—yes, 80—matches. The 43–37 breakdown (Navratilova on top) stands as statistical proof of the premier rivalry in the history of women's tennis.

U.S. Open resume: Winner in 1975, '76, '77, '78, '80, and '82. Finalist in 1979, '83, and '84.

THE LEGENDS
Ivan Lendl

We should have liked Ivan Lendl, but we didn't. On the record, he deserved our affection. He captured 94 singles titles, second only to Jimmy Connors (whom we esteemed beyond reason). He ran up the third-longest victory streak of the open era. Most endearingly, one would think, he overcame the tag "can't win the big ones" to win a bunch of big ones.

What was "wrong" with Lendl? Mainly that he looked and acted like a stiff. With his bullet-shaped head, accentuated by an odd haircut, he seemed to be a Prussian instead of the Czech he actually was. His demeanor didn't help: always somber, often sour, even when he was winning the match; judging by Lendl's expressions, playing championship tennis for

> ## "Lendl captured 94 singles titles, ran up the third-longest victory streak of the open era, and overcame the tag 'can't win the big ones' to win a bunch of big ones."

millions of dollars was no more enjoyable than working on an assembly line. In addition, he followed a rigid set of automaton-like mannerisms, particularly a set number of ball bounces before serving and studious picking of strings between points.

His style of play didn't help his image, either. Lendl pulverized people from the baseline and service line. He lacked confidence at the net—sometimes to the point that, given a short ball, he'd pull an Aaron Krickstein: pound it into a far corner and retreat toward the baseline, rather than charge the net for an anticipated putaway, as any decent club player would do.

Indeed, Lendl found volleying so unsettling you'd think he (like Krickstein) had graduated from Nick Bollettieri's Academy of Baseline Blasting. In fact, he learned to play that way in then-Czechoslovakia. Other Czechs of his era, notably Tomas Smid, were excellent volleyers, but not Lendl. Perhaps we should blame his parents, both of whom were nationally ranked.

The real reason was that Lendl found early on that he could win matches with his potent forehand and serve (the strong backhand came later), so why change? That style cost him one of his most coveted goals, a title at Wimbledon, where even a very big serve must be followed by an occasional good volley. He had one impressive stretch at Wimbledon—two straight runner-up finishes followed by three straight semifinals—but could not break through for the championship.

For a long while, that was the Lendl story at all the Grand Slam events. It took him seven years and four failed finals before he won his first, the French Open in 1984. He quickly grabbed two more titles in France and later two in Australia. But the U.S. Open bedeviled him and fed the idea that he would always be a bridesmaid. Between 1982 and '84, he lost three finals in succession, two to Connors, one to John McEnroe.

Then Lendl jammed his determination into overdrive—not with an artistic flair but with self-discipline. He undertook a regimen of physical training that would have crippled most people. He supplemented that with a high-carbo, high-fiber diet designed by Robert (*Eat to Win*) Haas—nearly revolutionary eating for tennis players in those days.

The new Lendl hit Flushing Meadows like a hurricane. In the 1985, '86, and '87 finals, he whipped McEnroe in three sets, fellow Czech Miloslav Mecir in three, and Mats Wilander in four. Although he still wasn't volleying much, he now had more stamina and mental toughness. Those titles satisfied his hunger for success, and they marked the high point of a career that then proceeded on a long, dignified descent.

But not even latter-day triumph made the public and media like Lendl. Nor did his applying for American citizenship (obtained in 1992), working with kids, smiling more, or suffering back problems that rule out play on the Champions tour. Old images die hard, no matter how flawed they may be.

U.S. Open resume: Winner in 1985, '86, and '87. Finalist in 1982, '83, '84, '88, and '89.

THE LEGENDS
John McEnroe

"[In] terms of tennis talent," wrote the astute Arthur Ashe, "I have never seen anyone better than John." But Ashe also bluntly criticized Mac for "boorish behavior" that "cost the sport" in terms of reputation. Therein lies the essential duality, and fascination, of John McEnroe's career.

In terms of sheer talent, it can be argued, nobody, not only Ashe, ever saw anyone better. McEnroe held the tennis patent on Muhammad Ali's ability to "float like a butterfly, sting like a bee." Deceptively quick and light on his feet, with superb anticipation, he glided into shots that most players had to lunge for, or never reached at all. But his primary hallmark, in an age when power began taking over tennis, was his judicious use of power. The consummate minimalist, Mac never over-swung at the ball or over-played a shot, preferring to hit it just hard enough to get the job done—a self-discipline that seems at odds with his high-strung tennis personality.

McEnroe at his best was probably the finest volleyer in history. At net especially, minimalism—coupled with precision—marked his play. He eschewed booming put-away attempts (and the errors they sometimes produce) in favor of adroit use of angles and perfect placements.

He invented his own stroking style that years of lessons did not change. No great player looks—or looked—as stiff and stick-like as John McEnroe. None hit—or hits—the ball like McEnroe: the short, straight backswing on ground strokes; the blocked, feathery volleys; above all, the signature service motion, with its extreme sideways stance and deep, gawky dip for the toss. From what well of individualism did such a style emerge? Not from the family. Brother Patrick McEnroe has played very well with a style that's as orthodox as it is graceful.

Although enough of a student to get admitted to Stanford, McEnroe stayed there just long enough to launch his run at pro tennis. What a start he made: from ranking No. 264 in 1976 to 21 in '77 and 4 in '78. By 1981, he was top dog, and he remained at the top for four consecutive years. His reign at the U.S. Open included four titles before Ivan Lendl, starting his own run at the Open, deprived McEnroe of a fifth. Three Wimbledon titles and a broad assortment of doubles victories were also his.

Only clay-court singles success eluded McEnroe, who rarely had enough patience to slog through a long slow-surface match. Still, he persevered for years at the French Open and played some memorable matches there. In 1984, he led Lendl two sets to zero before succumbing to his own foul temper and his characteristic lack of physical training.

Of that temper, and the unpleasant, embarrassing scenes it has produced on courts around the world,

> **"Deceptively quick and light on his feet, with superb anticipation, he glided into shots that most players had to lunge for, or never reached at all."**

little new can be said. On the available evidence, however, two points should be made: McEnroe seemed innately unable to act in a more mature, responsible manner; and opponents—even those who detested his behavior—seldom accused him of wielding it as a weapon for unsettling them.

McEnroe earns at least partial atonement for one thing: his singularly faithful participation in Davis Cup matches. In our time, players who are generally much more reliable than McEnroe routinely spurn entreaties to play for the oft-beleaguered U.S. team. McEnroe almost never did. He participated when asked, simply because he considered it both an honor and a duty, and U.S. fortunes rose accordingly. McEnroe played Davis Cup more years (12) and won more victories (41 in singles, 18 in doubles) than anyone else in this nation's history. Of that he should always feel proud.

U.S. Open resume: Winner in 1979, '80, '81, and '84. Finalist in 1985. Also won four men's doubles titles.

Martina Navratilova

Because she performed so gloriously through the middle and late years of her career, we tend to forget how difficult it was early on for Martina Navratilova. Not just in tennis, also in life: overweight and easily upset on court; homesick but eager to escape the Iron Curtain; unhappy with her sexual identity. Her ability to surmount all that, and to handle celebrity and anti-lesbian bigotry, was rooted in an early, innate determination to succeed.

As a child growing up in a distant suburb of Prague, far from Tennis Central of the time, Navratilova recalls that, "I knew one day I was going to be the best tennis player in the world." What a journey from Revnice, Czechoslovakia, to become the consensus choice for best woman player ever. (Margaret Smith Court and Steffi Graf—if she stays on course—are the only other serious contenders. The three have been champions repeatedly on all surfaces.)

What Navratilova did most of all over her two-decade-plus career was win. She won 167 singles and 165 doubles titles, as well as a few dozen others in Federation Cup and Wightman Cup play and exhibitions. With 56 Grand Slam tournament victories in singles, doubles, and mixed doubles, she trails only Court among women.

The Navratilova record is all the more impressive because it was compiled after a slow start. She made her tour debut in 1973, but did not win a major singles title until 1978; starting the 1982 season, she had only three.

Then her dammed-up talent burst through: 1982—French Open and Wimbledon; 1983—Australian Open, Wimbledon, U.S. Open; 1984—French, Wimbledon, U.S. By the end of the decade, she had won six more majors in singles and 36 all told in doubles. With her ninth singles victory at Wimbledon in 1990, she became the all-time leading singles winner there. Her four singles victories (in a five-year span) at the U.S. Open almost pale by comparison. In fact, the U.S. proved a source of relative frustration: Navratilova did not win there until her 11th try.

Meanwhile, however, she was consolidating her lock on the doubles. Navratilova's regular partner was Pam Shriver, and together they won 79 matches, including a record-tying 20 majors. Navratilova–Shriver was almost certainly the strongest women's pair in history, and Martina was the stronger of the strongest—further ammunition for those who consider her the best player.

Although it has long been considered a compliment to say that a certain woman played like a man, the phrase actually denigrates Navratilova. She played like Navratilova, with more touch and tactical skill (as well as gracefulness) than all but a few men. Cat-quick, beautifully balanced, impressively

> ## "What a journey from Revnice, Czechoslovakia, to become the consensus choice for best woman player ever."

athletic, she covered the court better than any other woman of any era. She also volleyed far better than anyone of her own era. Secure in the mind's eye: Navratilova, perfectly prepared, concentrating intently, slicing her left-handed, down-the-line backhand and taking the net for a deftly angled put-away.

How much greater than the others would she have been had she been more emotionally mature (and less overweight) in her early years as a professional? If she hadn't been distracted by the lure of defection and then by her inability to see her parents after she made her move to the West? If, if.... The upside is that frustrations and soaring successes made Navratilova, in the end, a most intelligent, perceptive, and human tennis champion, as nearly a female counterpart to Arthur Ashe as the game has yet produced.

U.S. Open resume: Winner in 1983, '84, '86, and '87. Also won nine women's and two mixed doubles titles.

FOURTH SET:

THE RECENT YEARS 1988–1996

FOURTH SET
The Recent Years
1988–1996

Aficionados of verve and personality in championship tennis worried as John McEnroe, Jimmy Connors, and Martina Navratilova departed the U.S. Open scene. The mantle seemed to be passing to stolid, unemotional types who cared about nothing but the bottom line, on the court as well as at the bank. Well, yes, Andre Agassi was different, but his image depended more on offcourt high life than dependable oncourt performance. Further, the worriers said, technology was taking over, and soon many men's matches and maybe some women's at the Open would resemble a bad day at Wimbledon: all serve plus a few volleys.

As the century drew to a close, both of those fears were turning out to be at the least exaggerated. To be sure, it proved hard to bid some of the older champions goodbye. Chris Evert and Connors, the former "lovebird double," went out in endearing ways. In the 1989 event, which she announced as her last, Evert gave 15-year-old Monica Seles a 6–0, 6–2 lesson. But then, against Zina Garrison, she lost a 5–2 first-set lead and won only three more games. Said a red-eyed Evert quietly, "I knew my last match here would be sad, win or lose." In 1991, his next-to-last year at the Open, Connors put on one of the splashy tennis shows of all time, swaggering his way into the semifinals with a series of improbable, high-pressure wins.

On came the new royalty: Agassi, Pete Sampras, Seles, Steffi Graf, and the usual supporting cast of princes, princesses, and pretenders. Agassi aside, proficiency-cum-dullness seemed to lie ahead. In fact, the only thing dull about this crowd was its oncourt behavior; nobody ranted and raved as Connors and McEnroe used to do, and professional tennis again became something like a decorous sport.

High drama surrounded both Seles (right), whose career was interrupted by a crazed fan in 1993, and Graf (left), whose personal problems became fodder for the tabloid press in Germany.

CLASSIC MATCHES

1992 SEMIFINAL: STEFAN EDBERG VERSUS MICHAEL CHANG

Here they were again, the French Open gladiators of '89, going the distance and then some: five hours, 26 minutes, a record for major tournaments. Given Edberg's fine serve-and-volley game, one could have expected a match of reasonable length. But not against Chang, the fiercest retriever around. For the fans, the match offered players with sharply contrasting styles. One statistic showed just how contrasting: In 60 games, Chang came to net on 70 occasions, Edberg on 254. Oddly, Edberg this day got little from his serve, winning a meager 51 percent of first-serve points. (Indeed, serves were hardly a factor: The match produced a monstrous 23 breaks.) The players split the first two sets after each had pulled up from 2–5 to tie the score. The third went to a tiebreak after Chang's barrage of backhand passing shots broke serve at 3–5. In the ensuing tiebreak, Edberg raced to a 6–0 lead before winning it 7–3. A backhand volley past the baseline gave Chang the service break he needed in set four, and four games later, he knotted the set score at two apiece. At crunch time, Edberg had greater reserves than Mr. Reserves. He also had history on his side: He'd won 10 of his 14 matches against Chang. This time he simply played solidly and got one more service break than his opponent. Result: 6–4 Edberg in the fifth.

1995 FINAL: STEFFI GRAF VERSUS MONICA SELES

This had to be the most oddly emotional big match ever played. Only a few weeks earlier, Seles had returned from her 28-month, stabbing-induced layoff (and had won all of her 11 matches). Because Seles's assailant was determined that Graf remain No. 1, Graf considered herself the unwitting cause of the stabbing. Understandably, the tennis was highly uneven. After a great first set, Graf, ahead but admittedly nervous, failed to win a game in the second. No trace of nerves in the third: Graf ratcheted up her serve, and, as Seles said later, returned drives that would have won points against lesser opponents. A single service break was all Graf needed to win, 7–6, 0–6, 6–3. At the umpire's stand, the two women hugged and kissed. For Graf, it was more than a Grand Slam victory. She felt a large burden of odd guilt lifted from her shoulders: Monica was back, playing, and playing very well.

As a group, again with Agassi an exception, they played consistently well and often brilliantly. And as human beings, they faced daunting personal problems and handled them by and large in impressive fashion.

The world knows what happened to Seles: stabbed by a German spectator during a changeover in Hamburg, Germany; out of the game completely, and a near-recluse, for more than two years; an up-and-down career, at least by her own standards, ever since.

Graf could be pardoned for thinking she'd been assaulted, too. She seemed constantly to be nursing injuries, but played through most of them. Worse, she was beset by all-too-public difficulties surrounding her and her father's financial affairs.

Sampras's troubles unfolded oncourt for everyone to see. His repsonse to them demonstrated his courage and humanity, and also showed how gripping championship tennis in late-summer New York can be. Sampras played at least two U.S. Open matches in a state of real physical illness. One was in 1994, against Jaime Yzaga. Weakened by several weeks of injury-induced inactivity, Sampras could no longer cope with long matches. His feet were blistered, his back aching. In the fifth set, he leaned on his racquet and looked like he'd collapse. After knotting the score at 5–all on the strength of sheer guts—"I wasn't going to give up"—Sampras went down to defeat. The crowd gave him a rousing ovation as warm as it was loud.

Sampras's second match-under-duress came in 1996, in the quarterfinals against Alex Corretja, when he became severely dehydrated and sick to his stomach. All but comatose in the fifth-set tiebreak, Sampras vomited behind the baseline, groaned audibly and beseeched the heavens, but somehow stayed in the points. Desperate to end the ordeal, he hit a hard second serve that caught Corretja off guard and rattled him enough for Sampras to pull out the victory.

There was the emotional challenge, in 1995–96, of playing while his coach and father figure, Tim Gullikson, was dying of brain cancer. Sampras never tried to hide his anguish from the public, including

the fans at the Open. In so doing, he gave pro tennis a touchingly human face.

Nobody ever knows how well or badly Agassi will perform, and different Agassis have shown up at Flushing Meadows. The best of those, Super-Andre, arrived unseeded in '94 and ripped through four seeded opponents before demolishing the fifth, Michael Stich, in a straight-set final. Whether he sports shaggy locks or a fuzzy-bald look, one ear-

ring or 20, Agassi, like the Open, is a New York happening: irreverent, glitz-loving, headline-making, pumped up by crowds and hoopla.

The loss of Seles, coupled with the premature quasi-retirement of the troubled Jennifer Capriati, dealt the women's game a hard blow. But except for 1993, the year of Seles' stabbing, the female side of the Open did not obviously suffer. By 1994, Arantxa Sánchez Vicario was picking up her game. Typecast

*Whether or not Agassi (left) appears at the Open in Super-Andre mode, he is always a charismatic presence; Hingis (right) should be making **her** presence felt for years to come.*

as a slow-court retriever, she took lessons in offense and mental toughness to break that mold. Those efforts paid off handsomely when Sánchez Vicario faced Graf in the '94 final. Losing the first set by 6–1 did not spell ultimate disaster. Sánchez Vicario toughed out a tiebreak second set and won the third, 6–4, to waltz into the U.S. Open winner's circle.

Since then, Graf has held the reins at Flushing. She defeated a resurgent Seles in a classic final in 1995 (see box, page 146) and again, in two close sets, the following year. Although Seles' stabbing created tension between her and Graf, and became a thorny issue throughout the women's tennis world, the two were now growing closer. At the end of the '95 match, they embraced and kissed on the cheek. Graf called it "great" to see her No. 1–rival "so at peace with herself."

At the same time, a fresh face and formidable talent—Martina Hingis—pushed into the picture. A phenom in the juniors, Hingis streaked up through the pro rankings. At the Open, she reached the fourth round in '95 and the semifinals (with wins over Sánchez Vicario and Jana Novotna) in '96. Hingis looked to be Evert-plus: strong ground strokes but more weapons overall and the tactical smarts to use them effectively.

Curiously, Hingis's tactics-based success hit Flushing Meadows amid a notable surge in the power game among women. The top speed of the women's first serves mounted each year (the current hard-ball champ, Brenda Schultz-McCarthy, has been clocked at 122 mph, which would have been considered a men's cannonball not long ago). The forehands hit by Graf and a few others could put some of their male counterparts on the defensive. Alloy racquets aside, an incessant quest for an edge against the competition seemed to be fueling the power boom.

What of the tournament itself? How does it now fare? From the evidence at hand, very well. Schultz-McCarthy and huge-serving Mark Philippoussis notwithstanding, power has not yet taken over the game. Commercially, the Open sets new paid attendance records each year, and VIPs of every stripe continue to watch and be watched. Even the grounds have been improved. The one-time concrete jungle now boasts thousands of flowers and other grace notes that make the ambience, if not serene, much more than tolerable.

Rx for Open success: Just keep rerouting those infernal airplanes, and let the rest—the buzz and the shouting, the glitz and the glory—stay as it is. New York has always done its own thing. Its tennis tournament should do that, too.

1988

The Era in Pictures 1988–1996

"A Slam is amazing, unbelievable. I don't care if it was against old ladies or everybody was sick."

–Ivan Lendl on
Steffi Graf's Grand Slam

The Open marks the coronation of the undisputed new queen of tennis as Steffi Graf (above), just 19, becomes the first player since Margaret Smith Court in 1970 to complete a Grand Slam. Graf defeats Gabriela Sabatini 6–3, 3–6, 6–1 in the final, then, with tennis reinstated as an Olympic sport, goes on to win a gold medal two months later in Seoul. Sweden's Mats Wilander (left) is the men's champion, beating Ivan Lendl 6–4, 4–6, 6–3, 5–7, 6–4 in a baseline battle that extends for four hours and 55 minutes, the longest U.S. singles final in the open era.

1989

CHAMPIONS

SINGLES
Boris Becker
Steffi Graf

DOUBLES
John McEnroe
& Mark Woodforde

Hana Mandlikova
& Martina Navratilova

MIXED DOUBLES
Robin White
& Shelby Cannon

"It's harder to play Ivan [Lendl] than Boris because Ivan's more consistent.... But if Becker's playing great, sorry, you have no chance."

—Andre Agassi

West Germany celebrates wildly as Boris Becker (right) and Steffi Graf (left) are the singles champions. In the women's draw, the symbolism of a generational shift is unmistakable: Graf defeats Martina Navratilova 3–6, 7–5, 6–1 in the final and Chris Evert plays her last Open match, losing to Zina Garrison in the quarterfinals. Becker defeats Ivan Lendl 7–6, 1–6, 6–3, 7–6 in a match that marks Lendl's record-tying eighth straight singles final appearance.

1990

Gabriela Sabatini (above), in her second Open finals appearance, ends a string of frustrating encounters with Steffi Graf by upsetting her 6–2, 7–6. In the men's draw, Pete Sampras, at 19 years old, becomes the youngest men's winner ever, defeating Andre Agassi in straight sets in the final. In women's doubles Gigi Fernandez (left, top) and Martina Navratilova beat Jana Novotna (near court, left) and Helena Sukova for Navratilova's ninth and final women's doubles title.

CHAMPIONS

SINGLES
Stefan Edberg
Monica Seles

DOUBLES
John Fitzgerald
& Anders Jarryd

Pam Shriver
& Natasha Zvereva

MIXED DOUBLES
Manon Bollegraf
& Tom Nijssen

Jim Courier (left) loses to Stefan Edberg in the men's final in straight sets, but the real drama in the men's draw centers around Jimmy Connors, who makes a final run at the title at the age of 39, surviving close matches with Patrick McEnroe and Aaron Krickstein to make the semis, where his dream is shattered by Courier. Monica Seles (above) wins her first Open, defeating Martina Navratilova 7–6, 6–1 for her third Grand Slam victory of the year.

1992

CHAMPIONS

SINGLES
Stefan Edberg
Monica Seles

DOUBLES
Jim Grabb
& Richey Reneberg

Gigi Fernandez
& Natasha Zvereva

MIXED DOUBLES
Nicole Provis
& Mark Woodforde

The ever-athletic Michael Chang (left) meets eventual champion Stefan Edberg in a memorable semifinal clash that Edberg wins, 6–7, 7–5, 7–6, 5–7, 6–4. The time of the match is five hours and 26 minutes, believed to be the longest contest in U.S. Open history. Monica Seles (right) is the champion again in the women's draw, winning her sixth Grand Slam event of the previous eight contested. Her run of success will be ended by a crazed fan who stabs her in the back in 1993, preventing her from playing in a major again until the 1995 Open.

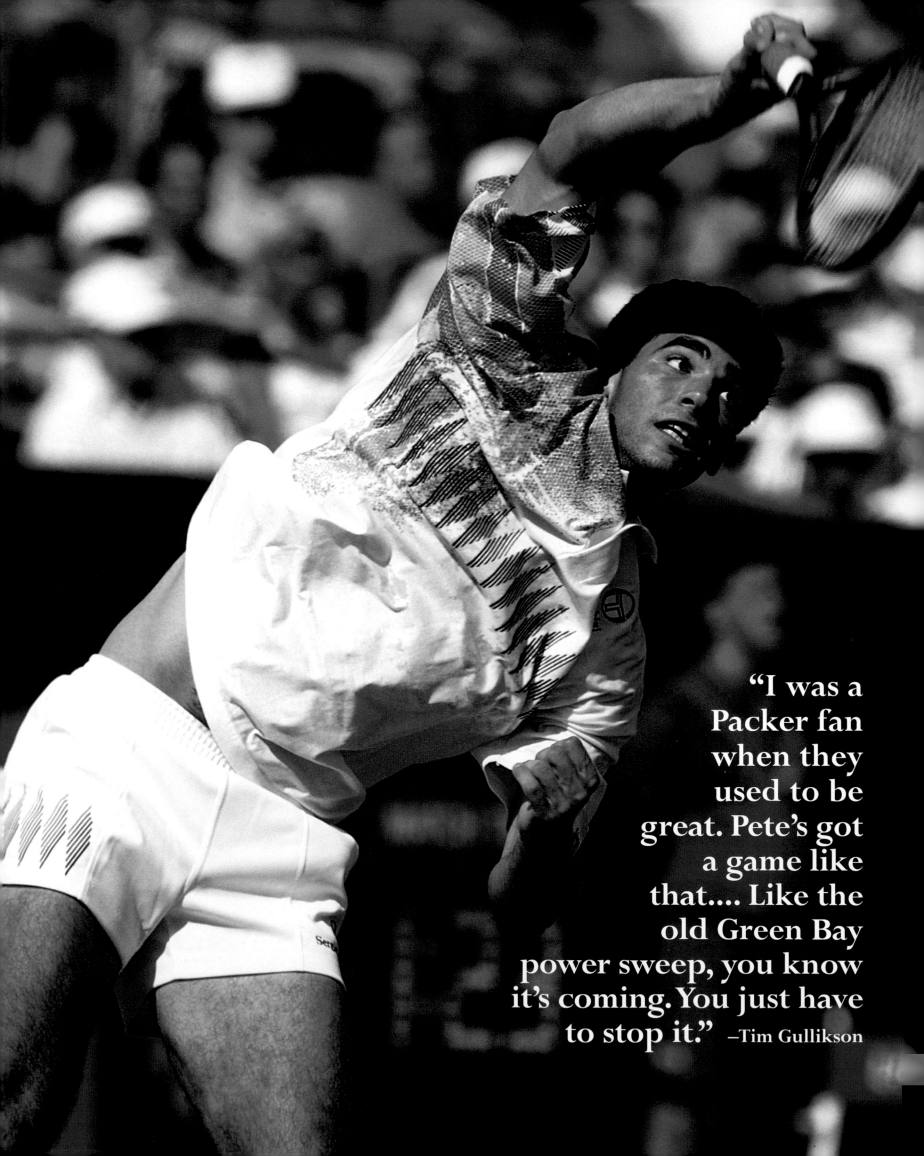

"I was a Packer fan when they used to be great. Pete's got a game like that.... Like the old Green Bay power sweep, you know it's coming. You just have to stop it." —Tim Gullikson

1993

CHAMPIONS

SINGLES
Pete Sampras
Steffi Graf

DOUBLES
Ken Flach
& Rick Leach

Arantxa Sánchez Vicario
& Helena Sukova

MIXED DOUBLES
Helena Sukova
& Todd Woodbridge

Pete Sampras (left) returns to championship form, easily disposing of Cédric Pioline in straight sets for his second Open singles title. In the women's competition, Monica Seles's absence produces new faces like Helena Sukova (right) in the later rounds, but the eventual winner is as familiar as they come: Steffi Graf barely dampens her headband in eliminating Sukova 6–3, 6–3 in the final.

1994

CHAMPIONS

SINGLES
Andre Agassi
Arantxa Sánchez Vicario

DOUBLES
Jacco Eltingh
& Paul Haarhuis

Jana Novotna
& Arantxa Sánchez Vicario

MIXED DOUBLES
Elna Reinach
& Patrick Galbraith

"When I won Wimbledon, it was a relief. Winning this one, I feel I've made a surge forward. There's a difference between saying, 'Wheeeww, I did it,' and saying 'Yes. I *can* do it.' "

—Andre Agassi

"To be part of walking on that court, it's a great feeling—it really is—to walk out with him. It's different. Andre's game . . . I have a lot of respect for it."

–Pete Sampras
on his rivalry with
Andre Agassi

1995

CHAMPIONS

SINGLES
Pete Sampras
Steffi Graf

DOUBLES
Todd Woodbridge
& Mark Woodforde

Gigi Fernandez
& Natasha Zvereva

MIXED DOUBLES
Meredith McGrath
& Matt Lucena

In what is fast becoming an out-standing rivalry, Pete Sampras (left) and defending champion Andre Agassi meet in the final, with Sampras winning his third

Open title 6–4, 6–3, 4–6, 7–5. But the match to watch is the women's final between Steffi Graf (above) and Monica Seles, who is playing in her first major since being stabbed

in 1993. The pair put on an exhi-bition of stirring tennis and superb sportsmanship as Graf wears Seles down in the third and decisive set. The final score: 7–6, 0–6, 6–3.

The tenacity of Michael Chang (left) finally gets him into an Open final, but the power of Pete Sampras is too much for him as Sampras, just 25, wins his fourth Open title. Steffi Graf *beats Monica Seles for her fifth Open championship, but must be wondering how long she can hold off future stars such as 15-year-old Martina Hingis (above), who loses to Graf in the semis.*

Andre Agassi

In Andre Agassi, tennis has its clearest example of the modern, ever-more-common blend of talent and entertainment value in today's society. Because he floats between those two, it's often hard to determine his real place in the game. Agassi's is a tough act to sustain, requiring a singlemindedness and self-discipline that he has so far not demonstrated.

We tend to judge Agassi by a higher standard. Why? Perhaps because he has such obvious skills. Both his forehand drive and service return (off both sides) belong in the category of all-time greats. Tennis people still talk about the way in which he handled Goran Ivanisevic's serve, among the fastest in the world, in the 1992 Wimbledon final. He can do that because his reaction time is second to none and because he has both a compact backswing and dazzling racquet-head speed.

Contrary to the views of some, Agassi also has intelligence and compassion. He established a charity to benefit children. He has been a dependable and highly successful Davis Cup player, with a record of straight singles wins (15) exceeded only by Bill Tilden (16). And without question, he has helped "grow the game," and tug it out of its prolonged doldrums, by making it attractive to a broader audience.

Raised in Las Vegas, little Andre was another of tennis's unending string of can't-miss four-year-olds. By 16, when he hit the tour, he could have knocked down Caesars Palace with his forehand. The rest of his game was rough. Tennis entrepreneur Nick Bollettieri, who had started working with Andre when he was 13, took on the task of smoothing it out. The Bollettieri Ground Stroke Academy refined his forehand, added a fine two-handed backhand and some other tools, but forgot to throw in a big-league serve and volley.

Still, Agassi's powerful if limited game carried him quickly aloft. In 1990, at age 20, he was runner-up at the U.S. and French Opens. Then came the stirring five-set victory over Ivanisevic and his cannon-balls at Wimbledon. At the same time, however, he was often losing in early rounds. In the spring of 1994, Agassi made a bold move. He hired as his coach Brad Gilbert, "Beej," a blue-collar guy whose playing career was winding down. Gilbert fused his work ethic and oncourt discipline with Agassi's talent, and the early results were explosive: five titles, including the U.S. Open, for the year; a leap in the rankings from 30-plus to 2.

Agassi surged through 1995, reaching 11 finals and winning seven of them. It looked as though he was really on the way to greatness. But 1996 brought another relapse: only two titles (in addition to Olympic gold), a first-round exit at Wimbledon,

> ## "Gilbert fused his work ethic with Agassi's talent and the results were explosive: five titles, including the U.S. Open, for the year...."

a second-round loss at the French; he even lost a match to doubles player/court jester Luke Jensen. What happened? Too much Brooke Shields as, at the '92 U.S. Open, there'd been too much Barbra Streisand? Too many commercials? Too many tempting substitutes for hard work, training, and attention to fitness? Too much self-absorption? Agassi became the most self-analyzing of all players, spinning theories about his angst, his goals, his you-name-it to anybody who'd listen. Some of the theories sounded sensible, others like psychobabble. But none seemed able to put him firmly on track.

At mid-career, therefore, it's uncertain whether this formidable talent will ever assert himself in a mature, dependable fashion. Perhaps his marriage to Shields will help. Still, as journalist Charlie Bricker observed in a profile of the man early in 1997, "the question is whether he has wasted his best years on Nike commercials instead of tennis."

U.S. Open resume: Winner in 1994. Finalist in '90 and '95.

Stefan Edberg

We don't often ascribe grace to a male tennis player. We talk instead about power, speed, endurance. In discussing Stefan Edberg, however, one can hardly ignore grace. Anyone who has watched Edberg maneuver on a court understands why. He moved like a dancer, with sure steps, a supple flow, a marvelous sense of balance. He was one of the best volleyers ever. The opponent's ball had to be within inches of the sideline to keep him from at least getting his racquet on it. And when it came low but within comfortable reach, he prepared for it like some Greek god of volleying: knees bent, head and shoulders down, racquet out front.

Coexisting oddly with this graceful style were two notably awkward strokes: serve and forehand. The Edberg serve featured a toss to an extreme point over the head and an even more extreme arching of the back. The forehand, as much a scoop as a stroke, began with an ungainly backswing that raised and cocked the elbow and pointed the racquet toward the net.

Both of these strokes generated skepticism among armchair critics. The service motion, they said, would lead to major back problems and shorten his career, while the forehand would always falter in pressure situations. The first never happened; the second, very seldom.

Edberg put together one of the premier attacking games of the past few decades. Yes, he could rally from backcourt, especially off the backhand, and he could win on clay; one of his last wins came against Michael Chang at the French Open in 1996. Yet he had a fast-court mentality: from the first stroke of any rally, he looked for an opening to come to the net.

Between the mid-1980s and early '90s, the most impressive stretch of his long career, Edberg reached the finals of at least one Grand Slam tournament each year save one. In 1990, despite a first-round exit at the U.S. Open, he gained the No. 1 ranking. He won the Open the following two years, dispatching America's best players, Jim Courier and Pete Sampras, by winning six of the total of seven sets.

Edberg had a special affinity for the Australian Open. In his 14 years on the tour, he skipped the Australian only once. He won it two times, the first of those in 1985, when his victory over Mats Wilander produced this memorable tableau of Swedish sportsmanship and camaraderie: victor and vanquished smiling broadly as they left the court together, Wilander's arm draped around his friend's shoulder.

Growing up in Sweden, Edberg set himself apart from the Bjorn Borg clones of that period. He devel-

> **"Edberg moved like a dancer, with sure steps, a supple flow, a marvelous sense of balance. He was one of the best volleyers ever."**

oped a serve-and-volley game, and he changed his backhand from a two-hander to a one-hander. His "heavy" second serve landed so consistently deep that he seemed literally to be aiming for the service line.

Edberg maintained the admirable Swedish trait of gentlemanly behavior. Yet he had a fiery streak, often pumping his fists, Connors-style, when he won big points and uttering a Swedish expletive when he lost them. (Of the expletive, he once told me with a grin, "It's not very nice, but it's not very loud.")

Despite that healthy emotional state, Edberg had to overcome a damaging psychological weakness: betraying his flagging spirits by hanging his head. His longtime coach, Tony Pickard, worked hard to banish that habit, telling his charge, "When you drop your head after losing a point, the guys at the top know you're down on yourself, and that may be just the edge they need to beat you." Edberg listened and learned, and he played hangdog no more.

U.S. Open resume: Winner in 1991 and '92.

Steffi Graf

If the mark of tennis greatness is the ability to win the biggest tournaments on a variety of surfaces—by expert reckoning, a fair definition—no women save Margaret Smith Court and Martina Navratilova have proved themselves as great as Steffi Graf. Since winning her first Grand Slam singles title in 1987, Graf has added 20 more. The distribution is as telling as the total: four Australian Opens (hard), five French Opens (clay), seven Wimbledons (grass), five U.S. Opens (hard).

And Graf, if her injury-prone body cooperates, still has several competitive years ahead. Only two outside forces, it seems, can stop her from overtaking Smith's record of 24 major singles titles. One is a fully rejuvenated Monica Seles. The other is teenaged Martina Hingis. Nobody else appears capable of winning more than an occasional match against Graf.

But Graf's story over the past few years has consisted of much more than glorious victories. It has been textured by emotional trials not of her making: the stabbing of Seles by a German fan determined to help Graf remain at the top; the trial and jailing of her father, Peter Graf, stemming from his mishandling of his daughter's tennis fortune.

One need not savor soap-opera scripts to appreciate the emotional significance of Graf's three-set victory over Seles in the 1995 U.S. Open. The spotlight shone principally on Seles, who played brilliantly in her first big event since returning to competition. But the match meant even more to Graf—less because she'd won another Grand Slam event over her principal rival than because their reappearance oncourt together lifted a terrible burden of guilt and remorse from Graf's shoulders. What had been done maniacally in her cause was now undone: Monica was back in competitive form again.

When Seles missed the final shot of that match, the two young women exchanged hugs and pecks on the cheek. Only their dignity and self-control, one supposes, kept them from weeping. Of course, Graf said later, it was important to defeat her resurgent rival. But "it's even more important to see her play that well and obviously enjoy herself and be . . . so at peace with herself. It's so great to see that."

In Seles's absence, Graf won six Grand Slam singles titles. It's easy to say, Yeah, but Seles wasn't there. Forget that. Even if the other team's best pitcher is on injured reserve, going six-for-nine is stunning. It's consistent with the kinds of records Graf has posted since she won that first, '87 Slam event, a three-set heartstopper over Navratilova in the French Open. That year, at ages 17 and 18, she lost only two of 77 matches.

Since then, aside from that six-for-nine, Graf has left these monuments along her trail: a Grand Slam

> ## "No women save Court and Navratilova have proved themselves as great as Graf ... and Graf still has several competitive years ahead."

(achieved previously by only Court and Maureen Connolly) in 1988; victories in three of the four majors in four different years; a record 186 straight weeks as No. 1—all before the attack on Seles; a 66-match winning streak, second longest of the open era; through '96, victory in at least seven tournaments a year for 11 years.

What's been the key to her success? For the first several years, the best forehand in women's history. Since then, a more reliable slice backhand, the addition of a top-spin backhand, and an improved serve-and-volley. All along, the ability to fight her way back from injuries or simply play through them. (A partial list includes back, thumb, calf, both feet, knee, with surgery required for the last two.) All along, the emotional strength to shove aside the kind of intrusions that threatened her in '96 and win, win, win.

U.S. Open resume: Winner in 1988, '89, '93, '95, and '96. Finalist in 1987, '90, and '94.

THE LEGENDS
Pete Sampras

In Pete Sampras, the U.S. has found a male tennis champion it can warmly embrace. Sampras makes it easy. He's modest, well-spoken, attractive. You don't have to make excuses for anything he does or says, and he keeps on winning. It's been a very long time since anyone else offered such a package.

Further, events have refashioned his original, drab personality. Whose heart wouldn't go out to a young man who shows his anguish during a Grand Slam quarterfinal because his coach was fighting for his life? Or to a man who battles his way through very-visible illness to finish, even win, his matches? Sampras has done all of that. He also has taken on just enough of the Connors/Navratilova, fist-clenching pugnaciousness to appeal to that side of the American nature.

Best of all about Sampras, we can be confident that he did none of the above in a calculated way. Things happened to Sampras, and he reacted as a decent, normal human being. It's almost enough to make one forget the many excesses of professional sport.

When Sampras came East from California to play in his first U.S. Open, he brought with him the oddest of home-grown coaches: Pete Fischer, a physician and very amateur player. Thing was, Fischer knew tennis, knew his young charge, and gave him an excellent grounding. Sampras began his pro career with a big serve and lots of raw talent. The rawness cooked quickly: After a lackluster first full season on the tour, he stunned the tennis world by winning the 1990 Open. The final against Andre Agassi was the first between U.S. men since 1979, and Sampras won in a walk. (Agassi, who has his lucid moments, later described it as "a good, old-fashioned street mugging.")

Sampras was a lot more prepared for Agassi than for what followed his triumph: shin splits, a shoulder injury, and unrelenting pressure. It took him a year to recover, and even in 1992 his best Grand Slam showing was runner-up (to Stefan Edberg) at the Open.

Then he hired former pro Tim Gullikson as his coach, and everything changed. "Gully" saw at once that Sampras was too dependent on his serve and too undisciplined in his approach to playing points. He convinced his pupil to emphasize other parts of his game, and showed him the value of playing "percentage" tennis—going for smart, makeable shots rather than flashy, difficult ones.

Sampras processed that advice into the most formidable all-court game of the decade. His ranking shot up to No. 1 in 1993 and has remained there almost ever since. Major titles tumbled in: three more U.S. Opens, three Wimbledons in succession, an Australian Open. Even so, it hasn't been a smooth path. Gullikson's death, of brain cancer in 1996,

> ## "[If] Sampras can acquire the endurance he needs . . . we may before long be hailing the best player in tennis history."

temporarily shattered Sampras. Chronic fatigue, apparently from an inherited form of anemia, caused him agonies oncourt and cost him matches in 1994 at Flushing Meadows and in '96 at Paris.

Can Sampras acquire the endurance he needs to complement his talent, tenacity, and match temperament? That's what he'll need to win the only big prize that has eluded him, the French Open. It has eluded other great U.S. players, too, including John McEnroe (who lost a two-set lead in the final) and Jimmy Connors (who never even made the finals). More than either of them, Sampras has the combination of strokes and strengths to conquer the slow clay that distinguishes the French from the other majors. He seems to have the patience and the willingness to change his game as well. If he does, and if he can endure long points during five-set matches, we may before long be hailing the best player in tennis history.

U.S. Open resume: Winner in 1990, '93, '95, and '96. Finalist in 1992.

THE LEGENDS
Monica Seles

Over the past couple of decades, the top echelon of women's tennis has witnessed as much tragedy or trouble as triumph: Players forced from the game by physical injury or emotional trauma; players beset by wayward or abusive fathers; and, of course, Monica Seles, stabbed by a lunatic bent on helping Steffi Graf become No. 1.

The Seles situation is the saddest. What happened to her owed nothing to her own actions or emotions, or to those of a relative. More than any of the others, she was victimized by the world we live in. And now, more than four years after the attack and two years after she returned from it, the question remains: Will Seles ever again be the player she was?

One can read the tangible evidence—match results—in two ways. On the negative side are a number of bad losses since the attack, including upsets by unknowns. On the positive side, a quick return to the late rounds of Grand Slam tournaments, where champions are judged: victory in the 1996 Australian Open; the finals in the '95 and '96 U.S. Open; the quarters in the '96 French Open; victory in five other events; and a rise in the rankings from 6th to 3rd during the first part of 1997.

Inevitably for Seles, there is another measure: how she fares against Graf, her chief rival since Seles hit the tour in 1989. Before the stabbing, Graf held a 6–4 advantage, but Seles had won two of the last three. Since then, Graf has won their two matches, both U.S. Open finals. Seles hung tough in each of them, however, the first a three-setter in which she took the second set at love.

If that in sum is a long way from dominance, it's also a long way from despair. Seles's problem now seems to be less Graf than two other factors: non-inflicted injuries and Martina Hingis. Since the stabbing, Seles has suffered a broken thumb and, of greater concern, a shoulder injury that may eventually require surgery. Hingis, the latest wunderkind, charged past both Seles and Graf to grab the No. 1 ranking in early '97. In the process, she beat Seles

in two finals: soundly at the '97 Lipton, narrowly at the '97 Hilton Head.

Yes, Seles played that Hilton Head match while suffering from the flu and took Hingis to a third-set tiebreak. On the other hand, Seles led 5–2 in the tiebreak before losing five straight points and the match. For a young woman who used to be the tour's toughest clutch player, that blown opportunity has to create angst.

There was already considerable angst. After the '96 season, Seles admitted that she lacked "feel" in her shots, a vital element to anybody who hits, as she does, all-out for winners. "Before," she

> ## "Will Seles ever again be the player she was?... [If not,] tennis will have lost more than a champion."

lamented, "the balls would be automatic. When I served or stroked the ball, I would know where it was going. Suddenly, I was not moving to the ball and didn't know where it was going."

We should all pray that the feel returns, along with concentration and the late-match killer instinct. They form the basis of Seles's game, and with less of each, she will never again be the player she was. If that happens, tennis will have lost more than a champion. Seles has given the entire sport a lift with her personality as well as her style of play. She is enthusiastic, outgoing, teenaged-giggly. On the deadly serious pro tours nowadays, everybody worries about results, rankings, and money. Seles provided relief from that.

The best sign of all may be the slightest: Close observers of the tour report that Seles has lost neither her love for the game nor her irrepressible giggle. Where there's giggling, there's hope.

U.S. Open resume: Winner in 1991 and '92. Finalist in 1995 and '96.

FIFTH SET
The Next Generation

Streaking supernovas: Australia's Mark Philippoussis (left), only 20 years old as of the 1997 Open, was already armed with a cannonball serve, while Martina Hingis (above) ascended to the No. 1 ranking at the age of 16.

American Dreams: Lindsay Davenport (above) showed her mettle by copping a gold in Atlanta in 1996; Justin Gimelstob (right) teamed with Chanda Rubin in 1997 to give the U.S. its first Hopman Cup.

Teen Angels: Venus Williams (left) is America's latest phenom—at 17 years of age as of the 1997 Open, her potential seemed limitless; Anna Kournikova (above) of Russia showed her promise when she reached the fourth round as a 15-year-old in 1996.

Dashing Duo: Chile's Marcelo Rios (above) cracked the top 10 at the age of 20; Chanda Rubin (right) of the U.S. won the 1997 Austrian Open—also as a 20-year-old—for her first WTA singles victory.

APPENDIX

NATIONAL MEN'S SINGLES FINALS

YEAR	CHAMPION	RUNNER-UP	SCORE
1881	Richard D. Sears	William E. Glyn	6-0, 6-3, 6-2
1882	Richard D. Sears	Clarence Clark	6-1, 6-4, 6-0
1883	Richard D. Sears	James Dwight	6-2, 6-0, 9-7
1884	Richard D. Sears	Howard Taylor	6-0, 1-6, 6-0, 6-2
1885	Richard D. Sears	Godfrey Brinley	6-3, 4-6, 6-0, 6-3
1886	Richard D. Sears	R. Livingston Beeckman	4-6, 6-1, 6-3, 6-4
1887	Richard D. Sears	Henry Slocum, Jr.	6-1, 6-3, 6-2
1888*	Henry Slocum, Jr.	Howard Taylor	6-4, 6-1, 6-0
1889	Henry Slocum, Jr.	Quincy Shaw	6-3, 6-1, 4-6, 6-2
1890	Oliver S. Campbell	Henry Slocum, Jr.	6-2, 4-6, 6-3, 6-1
1891	Oliver S. Campbell	Clarence Hobart	2-6, 7-5, 7-9, 6-1, 6-2
1892	Oliver S. Campbell	Frederick H. Hovey	7-5, 3-6, 6-3, 7-5
1893*	Robert D. Wrenn	Frederick H. Hovey	6-4, 3-6, 6-4, 6-4
1894	Robert D. Wrenn	Manliffe Goodbody	6-8, 6-1, 6-4, 6-4
1895	Frederick H. Hovey	Robert D. Wrenn	6-3, 6-2, 6-4
1896	Robert D. Wrenn	Frederick H. Hovey	7-5, 3-6, 6-0, 1-6, 6-1
1897	Robert D. Wrenn	Wilberforce V. Eaves	4-6, 8-6, 6-3, 2-6, 6-2
1898*	Malcolm D. Whitman	Dwight F. Davis	3-6, 6-2, 6-2, 6-1
1899	Malcolm D. Whitman	J. Parmly Paret	6-1, 6-2, 3-6, 7-5
1900	Malcolm D. Whitman	William A. Larned	6-4, 1-6, 6-2, 6-2
1901*	William A. Larned	Beals C. Wright	6-2, 6-8, 6-4, 6-4
1902	William A. Larned	Reggie F. Doherty	4-6, 6-2, 6-4, 8-6
1903	H. Laurie Doherty	William A. Larned	6-0, 6-3, 10-8
1904*	Holcombe Ward	William J. Clothier	10-8, 6-4, 9-7
1905	Beals C. Wright	Holcombe Ward	6-2, 6-1, 11-9
1906	William J. Clothier	Beals C. Wright	6-3, 6-0, 6-4
1907*	William A. Larned	Robert LeRoy	6-2, 6-2, 6-4
1908	William A. Larned	Beals C. Wright	6-1, 6-2, 8-6
1909	William A. Larned	William J. Clothier	6-1, 6-2, 5-7, 1-6, 6-1
1910	William A. Larned	Thomas C. Bundy	6-1, 5-7, 6-0, 6-8, 6-1
1911	William A. Larned	Maurice E. McLoughlin	6-4, 6-4, 6-2
1912†	Maurice E. McLoughlin	William F. Johnson	3-6, 2-6, 6-2, 6-4, 6-2
1913	Maurice E. McLoughlin	Richard N. Williams	6-4, 5-7, 6-3, 6-1
1914	Richard N. Williams	Maurice E. McLoughlin	6-3, 8-6, 10-8
1915	Bill Johnston	Maurice E. McLoughlin	1-6, 6-0, 7-5, 10-8
1916	Richard N. Williams	Bill Johnston	4-6, 6-4, 0-6, 6-2, 6-4
1917	R. Lindley Murray	Nat Niles	5-7, 8-6, 6-3, 6-3
1918	R. Lindley Murray	Bill Tilden	6-3, 6-1, 7-5
1919	Bill Johnston	Bill Tilden	6-4, 6-4, 6-3
1920	Bill Tilden	Bill Johnston	6-1, 1-6, 7-5, 5-7, 6-3
1921	Bill Tilden	Wallace F. Johnson	6-1, 6-3, 6-1
1922	Bill Tilden	Bill Johnston	4-6, 3-6, 6-2, 6-3, 6-4
1923	Bill Tilden	Bill Johnston	6-4, 6-1, 6-4
1924	Bill Tilden	Bill Johnston	6-1, 9-7, 6-2
1925	Bill Tilden	Bill Johnston	4-6, 11-9, 6-3, 4-6, 6-3
1926	Rene Lacoste	Jean Borotra	6-4, 6-0, 6-4
1927	Rene Lacoste	Bill Tilden	11-9, 6-3, 11-9
1928	Henri Cochet	Francis T. Hunter	4-6, 6-4, 3-6, 7-5, 6-3
1929	Bill Tilden	Francis T. Hunter	3-6, 6-3, 4-6, 6-2, 6-4
1930	John H. Doeg	Francis X. Shields	10-8, 1-6, 6-4, 16-14
1931	Ellsworth Vines	George M. Lott, Jr.	7-9, 6-3, 9-7, 7-5
1932	Ellsworth Vines	Henri Cochet	6-4, 6-4, 6-4
1933	Fred Perry	Jack Crawford	6-3, 11-13, 4-6, 6-0, 6-1
1934	Fred Perry	Wilmer L. Allison	6-4, 6-3, 1-6, 8-6
1935	Wilmer L. Allison	Sidney B. Wood	6-2, 6-2, 6-3
1936	Fred Perry	Don Budge	2-6, 6-2, 8-6, 1-6, 10-8
1937	Don Budge	Gottfried von Cramm	6-1, 7-9, 6-1, 3-6, 6-1
1938	Don Budge	Gene Mako	6-3, 6-8, 6-2, 6-1
1939	Bobby Riggs	Welby van Horn	6-4, 6-2, 6-4
1940	Don McNeill	Bobby Riggs	4-6, 6-8, 6-3, 6-3, 7-5
1941	Bobby Riggs	Francis Kovacs, 2nd	5-7, 6-1, 6-3, 6-3
1942	Ted Schroeder	Frank Parker	8-6, 7-5, 3-6, 4-6, 6-2
1943	Joseph R. Hunt	Jack Kramer	6-3, 6-8, 10-8, 6-0
1944	Frank Parker	William F. Talbert	6-4, 3-6, 6-3, 6-3
1945	Frank Parker	William F. Talbert	14-12, 6-1, 6-2
1946	Jack Kramer	Tom P. Brown	9-7, 6-3, 6-0
1947	Jack Kramer	Frank Parker	4-6, 2-6, 6-1, 6-0, 6-3
1948	Pancho Gonzales	Eric W. Sturgess	6-2, 6-3, 14-12
1949	Pancho Gonzales	Ted Schroeder	16-18, 2-6, 6-1, 6-2, 6-4
1950	Arthur Larsen	Herbie Flam	6-3, 4-6, 5-7, 6-4, 6-3
1951	Frank Sedgman	Vic Seixas	6-4, 6-1, 6-1
1952	Frank Sedgman	Gardnar Mulloy	6-1, 6-2, 6-3
1953	Tony Trabert	Vic Seixas	6-3, 6-2, 6-3
1954	Vic Seixas	Rex Hartwig	3-6, 6-2, 6-4, 6-4
1955	Tony Trabert	Ken Rosewall	9-7, 6-3, 6-3
1956	Ken Rosewall	Lew Hoad	4-6, 6-2, 6-3, 6-3
1957	Mal Anderson	Ashley J. Cooper	10-8, 7-5, 6-4
1958	Ashley J. Cooper	Mal Anderson	6-2, 3-6, 4-6, 10-8, 8-6
1959	Neale Fraser	Alex Olmedo	6-3, 5-7, 6-2, 6-4
1960	Neale Fraser	Rod Laver	6-4, 6-4, 9-7
1961	Roy Emerson	Rod Laver	7-5, 6-3, 6-2
1962	Rod Laver	Roy Emerson	6-2, 6-4, 5-7, 6-4
1963	Rafael Osuna	Frank Froehling, III	7-5, 6-4, 6-2
1964	Roy Emerson	Fred Stolle	6-4, 6-2, 6-4
1965	Manuel Santana	Cliff Drysdale	6-2, 7-9, 7-5, 6-1
1966	Fred Stolle	John Newcombe	4-6, 12-10, 6-3, 6-4
1967	John Newcombe	Clark Graebner	6-4, 6-4, 8-6

*No Challenge Round played. †Challenge Round abolished.

U.S. OPEN

YEAR	CHAMPION	RUNNER-UP	SCORE
1968	Arthur Ashe	Tom Okker	14-12, 5-7, 6-3, 3-6, 6-3
1969	Rod Laver	Tony Roche	7-9, 6-1, 6-2, 6-2
1970	Ken Rosewall	Tony Roche	2-6, 6-4, 7-6, 6-3
1971	Stan Smith	Jan Kodes	3-6, 6-3, 6-2, 7-6
1972	Ilie Nastase	Arthur Ashe	3-6, 6-3, 6-7, 6-4, 6-3
1973	John Newcombe	Jan Kodes	6-4, 1-6, 4-6, 6-2, 6-3
1974	Jimmy Connors	Ken Rosewall	6-1, 6-0, 6-1
1975	Manuel Orantes	Jimmy Connors	6-4, 6-3, 6-3
1976	Jimmy Connors	Bjorn Borg	6-4, 3-6, 7-6, 6-4
1977	Guillermo Vilas	Jimmy Connors	2-6, 6-3, 7-6, 6-0
1978	Jimmy Connors	Bjorn Borg	6-4, 6-2, 6-2
1979	John McEnroe	Vitas Gerulaitis	7-5, 6-3, 6-3
1980	John McEnroe	Bjorn Borg	7-6, 6-1, 6-7, 5-7, 6-4
1981	John McEnroe	Bjorn Borg	4-6, 6-2, 6-4, 6-3
1982	Jimmy Connors	Ivan Lendl	6-3, 6-2, 4-6, 6-4
1983	Jimmy Connors	Ivan Lendl	6-3, 6-7, 7-5, 6-0
1984	John McEnroe	Ivan Lendl	6-3, 6-4, 6-1
1985	Ivan Lendl	John McEnroe	7-6, 6-3, 6-4
1986	Ivan Lendl	Miloslav Mecir	6-4, 6-2, 6-0
1987	Ivan Lendl	Mats Wilander	6-7, 6-0, 7-6, 6-4
1988	Mats Wilander	Ivan Lendl	6-4, 4-6, 6-3, 5-7, 6-4
1989	Boris Becker	Ivan Lendl	7-6, 1-6, 6-3, 7-6
1990	Pete Sampras	Andre Agassi	6-4, 6-3, 6-2
1991	Stefan Edberg	Jim Courier	6-2, 6-4, 6-0
1992	Stefan Edberg	Pete Sampras	3-6, 6-4, 7-6, 6-2
1993	Pete Sampras	Cedric Pioline	6-4, 6-4, 6-3
1994	Andre Agassi	Michael Stich	6-1, 7-6, 7-5
1995	Pete Sampras	Andre Agassi	6-4, 6-3, 4-6, 7-5
1996	Pete Sampras	Michael Chang	6-1, 6-4, 7-6

NATIONAL WOMEN'S SINGLES FINALS

YEAR	CHAMPION	RUNNER-UP	SCORE
1887	Ellen Hansell	Laura Knight	6-1, 6-0
1888	Bertha L. Townsend	Ellen Hansell	6-3, 6-5
1889	Bertha L. Townsend	Louise D. Vorhees	7-5, 6-2
1890	Ellen C. Roosevelt	Bertha L. Townsend	6-2, 6-2
1891	Mabel Cahill	Ellen C. Roosevelt	6-4, 6-1, 4-6, 6-3
1892	Mabel Cahill	Elisabeth Moore	5-7, 6-3, 6-4, 4-6, 6-2
1893*	Aline Terry	Augusta Schultz	6-1, 6-3
1894	Helen Hellwig	Aline Terry	7-5, 3-6, 6-0, 3-6, 6-3
1895	Juliette Atkinson	Helen Hellwig	6-4, 6-2, 6-1
1896	Elisabeth Moore	Juliette Atkinson	6-4, 4-6, 6-2, 6-2
1897	Juliette Atkinson	Elisabeth Moore	6-3, 6-3, 4-6, 3-6, 6-3
1898	Juliette Atkinson	Marion Jones	6-3, 5-7, 6-4, 2-6, 7-5
1899*	Marion Jones	Maud Banks	6-1, 6-1, 7-5
1900*	Myrtle McAteer	Edith Parker	6-2, 6-2, 6-0
1901	Elisabeth Moore	Myrtle McAteer	6-4, 3-6, 7-5, 2-6, 6-2
1902	Marion Jones	Elisabeth Moore	6-1, 1-0 retired
1903	Elisabeth Moore	Marion Jones	7-5, 8-6
1904	May Sutton	Elisabeth Moore	6-1, 6-2
1905*	Elisabeth Moore	Helen Homans	6-4, 5-7, 6-1
1906*	Helen Homans	Maud Barger Wallach	6-4, 6-3
1907*	Evelyn Sears	Carrie Neely	6-3, 6-2
1908	Maud Barger Wallach	Evelyn Sears	6-3, 1-6, 6-3

Year	Champion	Runner-up	Score
1909	Hazel Hotchkiss	Maud Barger Wallach	6-0, 6-1
1910	Hazel Hotchkiss	Louise Hammond	6-4, 6-2
1911	Hazel Hotchkiss	Florence Sutton	8-10, 6-1, 9-7
1912*	Mary K. Browne	Eleanor Sears	6-4, 6-2
1913	Mary K. Browne	Dorothy Green	6-2, 7-5
1914	Mary K. Browne	Marie Wagner	6-2, 1-6, 6-1
1915*	Molla Bjurstedt	Hazel Hotchkiss Wightman	4-6, 6-2, 6-0
1916	Molla Bjurstedt	Louise Hammond Raymond	6-0, 6-1
1917*	Molla Bjurstedt	Marion Vanderhoef	4-6, 6-0, 6-2
1918	Molla Bjurstedt	Eleanor Goss	6-4, 6-3
1919†	Hazel Hotchkiss Wightman	Marion Zinderstein	6-1, 6-2
1920	Molla Bjurstedt Mallory	Marion Zinderstein	6-3, 6-1
1921	Molla Bjurstedt Mallory	Mary K. Browne	4-6, 6-4, 6-2
1922	Molla Bjurstedt Mallory	Helen Wills	6-3, 6-1
1923	Helen Wills	Molla Bjurstedt Mallory	6-2, 6-1
1924	Helen Wills	Molla Bjurstedt Mallory	6-1, 6-3
1925	Helen Wills	Kathleen McKane	3-6, 6-0, 6-2
1926	Molla Bjurstedt Mallory	Elizabeth Ryan	4-6, 6-4, 9-7
1927	Helen Wills	Betty Nuthall	6-1, 6-4
1928	Helen Wills	Helen Jacobs	6-2, 6-1
1929	Helen Wills	Phoebe Holcroft Watson	6-4, 6-2
1930	Betty Nuthall	Anna McCune Harper	6-1, 6-4
1931	Helen Wills Moody	Eileen Whitingstall	6-4, 6-1
1932	Helen Jacobs	Carolin Babcock	6-2, 6-2
1933	Helen Jacobs	Helen Wills Moody	8-6, 3-6, 3-0 retired
1934	Helen Jacobs	Sarah Palfrey	6-1, 6-4
1935	Helen Jacobs	Sarah Palfrey Fabyan	6-2, 6-4
1936	Alice Marble	Helen Jacobs	4-6, 6-3, 6-2
1937	Anita Lizana	Jadwiga Jedrzejowska	6-4, 6-2
1938	Alice Marble	Nancye Wynne	6-0, 6-3
1939	Alice Marble	Helen Jacobs	6-0, 8-10, 6-4
1940	Alice Marble	Helen Jacobs	6-2, 6-3
1941	Sarah Palfrey Cooke	Pauline Betz	7-5, 6-2
1942	Pauline Betz	Louise Brough	4-6, 6-1, 6-4
1943	Pauline Betz	Louise Brough	6-3, 5-7, 6-3
1944	Pauline Betz	Margaret Osborne	6-3, 8-6
1945	Sarah Palfrey Cooke	Pauline Betz	3-6, 8-6, 6-4
1946	Pauline Betz	Doris Hart	11-9, 6-3
1947	Louise Brough	Margaret Osborne	8-6, 4-6, 6-1
1948	Margaret Osborne duPont	Louise Brough	4-6, 6-4, 15-13
1949	Margaret Osborne duPont	Doris Hart	6-4, 6-1
1950	Margaret Osborne duPont	Doris Hart	6-3, 6-3
1951	Maureen Connolly	Shirley Fry	6-3, 1-6, 6-4
1952	Maureen Connolly	Doris Hart	6-3, 7-5
1953	Maureen Connolly	Doris Hart	6-2, 6-4
1954	Doris Hart	Louise Brough	6-8, 6-1, 8-6
1955	Doris Hart	Patricia Ward	6-4, 6-2
1956	Shirley Fry	Althea Gibson	6-3, 6-4
1957	Althea Gibson	Louise Brough	6-3, 6-2
1958	Althea Gibson	Darlene Hard	3-6, 6-1, 6-2
1959	Maria Bueno	Christine Truman	6-1, 6-4
1960	Darlene Hard	Maria Bueno	6-4, 10-12, 6-4
1961	Darlene Hard	Ann Haydon	6-3, 6-4
1962	Margaret Smith	Darlene Hard	9-7, 6-4
1963	Maria Bueno	Margaret Smith	7-5, 6-4
1964	Maria Bueno	Carole Graebner	6-1, 6-0
1965	Margaret Smith	Billie Jean Moffitt	8-6, 7-5
1966	Maria Bueno	Nancy Richey	6-3, 6-1
1967	Billie Jean King	Ann Haydon Jones	11-9, 6-4

*No Challenge Round played. †Challenge Round abolished.

U.S. Open

Year	Champion	Runner-up	Score
1968	Virginia Wade	Billie Jean King	6-4, 6-4
1969	Margaret Smith Court	Nancy Richey	6-2, 6-2
1970	Margaret Smith Court	Rosie Casals	6-2, 2-6, 6-1
1971	Billie Jean King	Rosie Casals	6-4, 7-6
1972	Billie Jean King	Kerry Melville	6-3, 7-5
1973	Margaret Smith Court	Evonne Goolagong	7-6, 5-7, 6-2
1974	Billie Jean King	Evonne Goolagong	3-6, 6-3, 7-5
1975	Chris Evert	Evonne Goolagong	5-7, 6-4, 6-2
1976	Chris Evert	Evonne Goolagong	6-3, 6-0
1977	Chris Evert	Wendy Turnbull	7-6, 6-2
1978	Chris Evert	Pam Shriver	7-5, 6-4
1979	Tracy Austin	Chris Evert Lloyd	6-4, 6-3
1980	Chris Evert Lloyd	Hana Mandlikova	5-7, 6-1, 6-1
1981	Tracy Austin	Martina Navratilova	1-6, 7-6, 7-6
1982	Chris Evert Lloyd	Hana Mandlikova	6-3, 6-1
1983	Martina Navratilova	Chris Evert Lloyd	6-1, 6-3

Year	Champion	Runner-up	Score
1984	Martina Navratilova	Chris Evert Lloyd	4-6, 6-4, 6-4
1985	Hana Mandlikova	Martina Navratilova	7-6, 1-6, 7-6
1986	Martina Navratilova	Helena Sukova	6-3, 6-2
1987	Martina Navratilova	Steffi Graf	7-6, 6-1
1988	Steffi Graf	Gabriela Sabatini	6-3, 3-6, 6-1
1989	Steffi Graf	Martina Navratilova	3-6, 7-5, 6-1
1990	Gabriela Sabatini	Steffi Graf	6-2, 7-6
1991	Monica Seles	Martina Narvatilova	7-6, 6-1
1992	Monica Seles	Arantxa Sánchez Vicario	6-3, 6-3
1993	Steffi Graf	Helena Sukova	6-3, 6-3
1994	Arantxa Sánchez Vicario	Steffi Graf	1-6, 7-6, 6-4
1995	Steffi Graf	Monica Seles	7-6, 0-6, 6-3
1996	Steffi Graf	Monica Seles	7-5, 7-4

NATIONAL MEN'S DOUBLES FINALS

Year	Champions	Runners-up	Score
1881	C. Clark - F. Taylor	A. Van Rensselaer - A. Newbold	6-5, 6-4, 6-5
1882	R. Sears - J. Dwight	W. Nightingale - G. Smith	6-2, 6-4, 6-4
1883	R. Sears - J. Dwight	A. Van Rensselaer - A. Newbold	6-0, 6-2, 6-2
1884	R. Sears - J. Dwight	A. Van Rensselaer - W. Berry	6-4, 6-1, 8-10, 6-4
1885	R. Sears - J. Clark	H. Slocum, Jr. - W. Knapp	6-3, 6-0, 6-2
1886	R. Sears - J. Dwight	H. Taylor - G. Brinley	7-5. 5-7, 7-5, 6-4
1887	R. Sears - J. Dwight	H. Taylor - H. Slocum, Jr.	6-4, 3-6, 2-6, 6-3, 6-3
1888	O. Campbell - V. Hall	C. Hobart - E. MacMullen	6-4, 6-2, 6-4
1889	H. Slocum, Jr. - H. Taylor	V. Hall - O. Campbell	6-1, 6-3, 6-2
1890	V. Hall - C. Hobart	J. Carver - J. Ryerson	6-3, 4-6, 6-2, 2-6, 6-3
1891	O. Campbell - R. Huntington, Jr.	V. Hall - C. Hobart	6-3, 6-4, 8-6
1892	O. Campbell - R. Huntington, Jr.	V. Hall - E. Hall	6-4, 6-2, 4-6, 6-2
1893	C. Hobart - F. Hovey	O. Campbell - R. Huntington, Jr.	6-3, 6-4, 4-6, 6-2
1894	C. Hobart - F. Hovey	C. Neel - S. Neel	6-3, 8-6, 6-1
1895	M. Chace - R. Wrenn	C. Hobart - F. Hovey	7-5, 6-1, 8-6
1896	C. Neel - S. Neel	R. Wrenn - M. Chase	6-3, 1-6, 6-1, 3-6, 6-1
1897	L. Ware - G. Sheldon, Jr.	H. Mahony - H. Nisbet	11-13, 6-2, 9-7, 1-6, 6-1
1898	L. Ware - G. Sheldon, Jr.	H. Ward - D. Davis	1-6, 7-5, 6-4, 4-6, 7-5
1899	H. Ward - D. Davis	L. Ware - G. Sheldon, Jr.	6-4, 6-4, 6-3
1900	H. Ward - D. Davis	F. Alexander - R. Little	6-4, 9-7, 12-10
1901	H. Ward - D. Davis	L. Ware - B. Wright	6-3, 9-7, 6-1
1902	R. Doherty - H. Doherty	H. Ward - D. Davis	11-9, 12-10, 6-4
1903	R. Doherty - H. Doherty	K. Collins - L. H. Waidner	7-5, 6-3, 6-3
1904	H. Ward - B. Wright	K. Collins - R. Little	1-6, 6-2, 3-6, 6-4, 6-1
1905	H. Ward - B. Wright	F. Alexander - H. Hackett	6-4, 6-4, 6-1
1906	H. Ward - B. Wright	F. Alexander - H. Hackett	6-3, 3-6, 6-3, 6-3
1907	F. Alexander - H. Hackett	N. Thornton - B. M. Grant	6-2, 6-1, 6-1
1908	F. Alexander - H. Hackett	R. Little - B. Wright	6-1, 7-5, 6-2
1909	F. Alexander - H. Hackett	M. McLoughlin - G. Janes	6-4, 6-4, 6-0
1910	F. Alexander - H. Hackett	T. Bundy - T. Hendrick	6-1, 8-6, 6-3
1911	R. Little - G. Touchard	F. Alexander - H. Hackett	7-5, 13-15, 6-2, 6-4
1912	M. McLoughlin - T. Bundy	R. Little - G. Touchard	3-6, 6-2, 6-1, 7-5
1913	M. McLoughlin - T. Bundy	J. Strachan - C. Griffin	6-4, 7-5, 6-1
1914	M. McLoughlin - T. Bundy	G. Church - D. Mathey	6-4, 6-2, 6-4
1915	W. Johnston - C. Griffin	M. McLoughlin - T. Bundy	2-6, 6-3, 6-4, 36-, 6-3
1916	W. Johnston - C. Griffin	M. McLoughlin - W. Dawson	6-4, 6-3, 5-7, 6-3
1917	F. Alexander - H. Throckmorton	H. Johnson - I. Wright	11-9, 6-4, 6-4
1918	W. Tilden - V. Richards	F. Alexander - B. Wright	6-3, 6-4, 3-6, 2-6, 6-2
1919	N. Brookes - G. Patterson	W. Tilden - V. Richards	8-6, 6-3, 4-6, 4-6, 6-2
1920	W. Johnston - C. Griffin	W. Davis - R. Roberts	6-2, 6-2, 6-3
1921	W. Tilden - V. Richards	R. Williams - W. Washburn	13-11, 12-10, 6-1
1922	W. Tilden - V. Richards	G. Patterson - P. O'Hara Wood	4-6, 6-1, 6-3, 6-4
1923	W. Tilden - B. Norton	R. Williams - W. Washburn	3-6, 6-2, 6-3, 5-7, 6-2
1924	H. Kinsey - R. Kinsey	G. Patterson - P. O'Hara Wood	7-5, 5-7, 7-9, 6-3, 6-4
1925	R. Williams - V. Richards	G. Patterson - J. Hawkes	6-2, 8-10, 6-4, 11-9
1926	R. Williams - V. Richards	W. Tilden - A. Chapin, Jr.	6-4, 6-8, 11-9, 6-3
1927	W. Tilden - F. Hunter	W. Johnston - R. Williams	10-8, 6-3, 6-3
1928	G. Lott, Jr. - J. Hennessey	G. Patterson - J. Hawkes	6-2, 6-1, 6-2
1929	G. Lott, Jr. - J. Doeg	B. Bell - L. White	10-8, 16-14, 6-1
1930	G. Lott, Jr. - J. Doeg	J. Van Ryn - W. Allison	8-6, 6-3, 3-6, 13-15, 6-4
1931	W. Allison - J. Van Ryn	G. Mangin - B. Bell	6-4, 6-3, 6-2
1932	H. E. Vines - K. Gledhill	W. Allison - John Van Ryn	6-4, 6-3, 6-2
1933	G. Lott, Jr. - L. Stoefen	F. Shields - F. Parker	11-13, 9-7, 9-7, 6-3
1934	G. Lott, Jr. - L. Stoefen	W. Allison - J. Van Ryn	6-4, 9-7, 3-6, 6-4
1935	W. Allison - J. Van Ryn	J. D. Budge - C. G. Mako	6-2, 6-3, 2-6, 3-6, 6-1
1936	J. D. Budge - C. G. Mako	W. Allison - J. Van Ryn	6-4, 6-2, 6-4
1937	G. von Cramm - H. Henkel	J. D. Budge - C. G. Mako	6-4, 7-5, 6-4
1938	J. D. Budge - C. G. Mako	A. Quist - J. Bromwich	6-3, 6-2, 6-1
1939	A. Quist - J. Bromwich	J. Crawford - H. Hopman	8-6, 6-1, 6-4
1940	J. Kramer - F. Schroeder	G. Mulloy - H. Prussoff	6-4, 8-6, 9-7
1941	J. Kramer - F. Schroeder	W. Sabin - G. Mulloy	9-7, 6-4, 6-2

Year	Champions	Runners-up	Score
1942	G. Mulloy - W. Talbert	F. Schroeder - S. Wood	9-7, 7-5, 6-1
1943	J. Kramer - F. Parker	W. Talbert - D. Freeman	6-2, 6-4, 6-4
1944	W. D. McNeill - R. Falkenburg	W. Talbert - F. Segura	7-5, 6-4, 3-6, 6-1
1945	G. Mulloy - W. Talbert	R. Falkenburg - J. Tuero	12-10, 8-10, 12-10, 6-2
1946	G. Mulloy - W. Talbert	D. McNeill - F. Guernsey	3-6, 6-4, 2-6, 6-3, 20-18
1947	J. Kramer - F. Schroeder	W. Talbert - W. Sidwell	6-4, 7-5, 6-3
1948	G. Mulloy - W. Talbert	F. Parker - F. Schroeder	1-6, 9-7, 6-3, 3-6, 9-7
1949	J. Bromwich - W. Sidwell	F. Sedgman - G. Worthington	6-4, 6-0, 6-1
1950	J. Bromwich - F. Sedgman	W. Talbert - G. Mulloy	7-5, 8-6, 3-6, 6-1
1951	K. McGregor - F. Sedgman	D. Candy - M. Rose	10-8, 6-4, 4-6, 7-5
1952	M. Rose - E. V. Seixas	K. McGregor - F. Sedgman	3-6, 1-8, 1-8, 6-8, 8-6
1953	R. Hartwig - M. Rose	G. Mulloy - W. Talbert	6-4, 4-6, 6-2, 6-4
1954	E. V. Seixas - T. Trabert	L. Hoad - K. Rosewall	3-6, 6-4, 8-6, 6-3
1955	K. Kamo - A. Miyagi	G. Moss - W. Quillian	6-3, 6-3, 3-6, 1-6, 6-4
1956	L. Hoad - K. Rosewall	H. Richardson - E. V. Seixas	6-2, 6-2, 3-6, 6-4
1957	A. Cooper - N. Fraser	G. Mulloy - J. E. Patty	4-6, 6-3, 9-7, 6-3
1958	A. Olmedo - H. Richardson	S. Giammalva - B. MacKay	3-6, 6-3, 6-4, 6-4
1959	N. Fraser - R. Emerson	A. Olmedo - E. Buchholz, Jr.	3-6, 6-3, 5-7, 6-4, 7-5
1960	N. Fraser - R. Emerson	R. Laver - R. Mark	9-7, 6-2, 6-4
1961	C. McKinley - D. Ralston	R. Osuna - A. Palafox	6-3, 6-4, 2-6, 13-11
1962	R. Osuna - A. Palafox	C. McKinley - D. Ralston	6-2, 10-12, 1-6, 9-7, 6-3
1963	C. McKinley - D. Ralston	R. Osuna - A. Palafox	9-7, 4-6, 5-7, 6-3, 11-9
1964	C. McKinley - D. Ralston	G. Stilwell - M. Sangster	6-3, 6-2, 6-4
1965	R. Emerson - F. Stolle	F. Froehling, III - C. Pasarell	6-4, 10-12, 7-5, 7-3
1966	R. Emerson - F. Stolle	C. Graebner - D. Ralston	6-4, 6-4, 6-4
1967	J. Newcombe - T. Roche	W. Bowrey - O. Davidson	6-8, 9-7, 6-3, 6-3

U.S. OPEN

Year	Champions	Runners-up	Score
1968	R. Lutz - S. Smith	A. Ashe - A. Gimeno	11-9, 6-1, 7-5
1969	K. Rosewall - F. Stolle	C. Pasarell - D. Ralston	2-6, 7-5, 13-11, 6-3
1970	P. Barthes - N. Pilic	R. Emerson - R. Laver	6-3, 7-6, 4-6, 7-6
1971	J. Newcombe - R. Taylor	S. Smith - E. van Dillen	6-7, 6-3, 7-6, 4-6, 7-6
1972	C. Drysdale - R. Taylor	O. Davidson - J. Newcombe	6-4, 7-6, 6-3
1973	O. Davidson - J. Newcombe	R. Laver - K. Rosewall	7-5, 2-6, 7-5, 7-5
1974	R. Lutz - S. Smith	P. Cornejo - J. Fillol	6-3, 6-3
1975	J. Connors - I. Nastase	T. Okker - M. Riessen	6-4, 7-6
1976	M. Riessen - T. Okker	P. Kronk - C. Letcher	6-4, 6-4
1977	B. Hewitt - F. McMillan	B. Gottfried - R. Ramirez	6-4, 6-0
1978	R. Lutz - S. Smith	M. Riessen - S. Stewart	1-6, 7-5, 6-3
1979	J. McEnroe - P. Fleming	R. Lutz - S. Smith	6-2, 6-4
1980	R. Lutz - S. Smith	J. McEnroe - P. Fleming	7-6, 3-6, 6-1, 3-6, 6-3
1981	J. McEnroe - P. Fleming	H. Gunthardt - P. McNamara	default
1982	K. Curren - S. Denton	V. Amaya - H. Pfister	6-2, 6-7, 5-7, 6-2, 6-4
1983	J. McEnroe - P. Fleming	F. Buehning - V. Winitsky	6-3, 6-4, 6-2
1984	J. Fitzgerald - T. Smid	S. Edberg - A. Jarryd	7-6, 6-3, 6-3
1985	K. Flach - R. Seguso	H. Leconte - Y. Noah	6-7, 7-6, 7-6, 6-0
1986	A. Gomez - S. Zivojinovic	J. Nystrom - M. Wilander	4-6, 6-3, 6-3, 4-6, 6-3
1987	S. Edberg - A. Jarryd	K. Flach - R. Seguso	7-6, 6-2, 4-6, 5-6, 7-6
1988	S. Casal - E. Sánchez	R. Leach - J. Pugh	walkover
1989	J. McEnroe - M. Woodforde	K. Flach - R. Seguso	6-4, 4-6, 6-3, 6-3
1990	P. Aldrich - D. Visser	P. Annacone - D. Wheaton	6-2, 7-6, 6-2
1991	J. Fitzgerald - A. Jarryd	S. Davis - D. Pate	6-3, 3-6, 6-3, 6-3
1992	J. Grabb - R. Reneberg	K. Jones - R. Leach	3-6, 7-6, 6-3, 6-3
1993	K. Flach - R. Leach	M. Damm - K. Novacek	6-7, 6-4, 6-2
1994	J. Eltingh - P. Haarhuis	T. Woodbridge - M. Woodforde	6-3, 8-6
1995	T. Woodbridge - M. Woodforde	A. O'Brien - S. Stolle	6-3, 6-3
1996	T. Woodbridge - M. Woodforde	P. Haarhuis - J. Eltingh	4-6, 7-6, 7-6

NATIONAL WOMEN'S DOUBLES FINALS

Year	Champions	Runners-up	Score
1889	M. Ballard - B. Townsend	M. Wright - L. Knight	6-0, 6-2
1890	E. Roosevelt - G. Roosevelt	B. Townsend - M. Ballard	6-1, 6-2
1891	M. Cahill - E. L. Morgan	G. Roosevelt - E. Roosevelt	2-6, 8-6, 6-4
1892	M. Cahill - A. McKinlay	H. D. Harris - A. Williams	6-1, 6-3
1893	A. Terry - H. Butler	A. Schultz - Miss Stone	6-4, 6-3
1894	H. Hellwig - J. Atkinson	A. Wistar - Amy Williams	6-4, 8-6, 6-2
1895	H. Hellwig - J. Atkinson	Elisabeth Moore - Amy Williams	6-2, 6-2, 12-10
1896	E. Moore - J. Atkinson	A. Wistar - Amy Williams	6-4, 7-5
1897	J. Atkinson - K. Atkinson	Mrs. F. Edwards - E. Rastall	6-2, 6-1, 6-1
1898	J. Atkinson - K. Atkinson	Marie Wimer - Carrie Neely	6-1, 2-6, 4-6, 6-1, 6-2
1899	J. Craven - Myrtle McAteer	Maud Banks - E. Rastall	6-1, 6-1, 7-5
1900	E. Parker - H. Champlin	Marie Wimer - Myrtle McAteer	9-7, 6-2, 6-2
1901	J. Atkinson - Myrtle McAteer	M. Jones - Elisabeth Moore	default
1902	J. Atkinson - Marion Jones	Maud Banks - N. Closterman	6-2, 7-5
1903	E. Moore - Carrie Neely	Miriam Hall - Marion Jones	6-4, 6-1, 6-1
1904	May Sutton - Miriam Hall	Elisabeth Moore - Carrie Neely	3-6, 6-3, 6-3
1905	Helen Homans - Carrie Neely	M. Oberteuffer - Virginia Maule	6-0, 6-1
1906	A. B. Coe - Mrs. D. Platt	Helen Homans - Clover Boldt	6-4, 6-4
1907	Marie Wimer - Carrie Neely	Edna Wildey - Natalie Wildey	6-1, 2-6, 6-4

Year	Champions	Runners-up	Score
1908	Evelyn Sears - Margaret Curtis	Carrie Neely - Marion Steever	6-3, 5-7, 9-7
1909	Hazel Hotchkiss - Edith Rotch	Dorothy Green - Lois Moyes	6-1, 6-1
1910	Hazel Hotchkiss - Edith Rotch	Adelaide Browning - Edna Wildey	6-4, 6-4
1911	Hazel Hotchkiss - Eleonora Sears	Dorothy Green - Florence Sutton	6-4, 4-6, 6-2
1912	D. Green - M. K. Browne	M. Barger-Wallach - Mrs. F. Schmitz	6-2, 5-7, 6-0
1913	M. K. Browne - L. Williams	Dorothy Green - Edna Wildey	12-10, 2-6, 6-3
1914	M. K. Browne - L. Williams	L. H. Raymond - Edna Wildey	8-6, 6-2
1915	Hazel H. Wightman - El. Sears	H. H. McLean - Mrs. G. L. Chapman	10-8, 6-2
1916	Molla Bjurstedt - El. Sears	L. H. Raymond - Edna Wildey	4-6, 6-4, 10-8
1917	Molla Bjurstedt - El. Sears	Phyllis Walsh - Mrs. R. LeRoy	6-2, 6-4
1918	M. Zinderstein - E. Goss	Molla Bjurstedt - Mrs. J. Rogge	7-5, 8-6
1919	M. Zinderstein - E. Goss	Eleonor Sears - Hazel H. Wightman	10-8, 9-7
1920	M. Zinderstein - E. Goss	E. Tennant - H. Baker	6-3, 6-1
1921	M. K. Browne - Mrs. R. Williams	H. Gilleaudeau - Mrs. L. G. Morris	6-3, 6-2
1922	M. Z. Jessup - Helen Wills	E. Sigourney - Molla B. Mallory	6-4, 7-9, 6-3
1923	K. McKane - P. H. Covell	Hazel H. Wightman - E. Goss	2-6, 6-2, 6-1
1924	Hazel H. Wightman - H. Wills	E. Goss - M. Z. Jessup	6-4, 6-3
1925	M. K. Browne - Helen Wills	May S. Bundy - Elizabeth Ryan	6-4, 6-3
1926	Elizabeth Ryan - E. Goss	M. K. Browne - C. H. Chapin	3-6, 6-4, 12-10
1927	K. M. Godfree - E. Harvey	Betty Nuthall - Joan Fry	6-1, 4-6, 6-4
1928	Hazel H. Wightman - H. Wills	Edith Cross - Anna McCune Harper	6-2, 6-2
1929	P. Watson - P. Michell	P. H. Covell - D. Shepherd-Barron	2-6, 6-3, 6-4
1930	B. Nuthall - S. Palfrey	Edith Cross - Anna McCune Harper	3-6, 6-3, 7-5
1931	B. Nuthall - E. B. Whitingstall	Helen Jacobs - Dorothy Round	6-2, 6-4
1932	Helen Jacobs - Sarah Palfrey	Edith Cross - Anna McCune Harper	3-6, 6-3, 7-5
1933	Betty Huthall - Freda James	H. Wills Moody - Elizabeth Ryan	default
1934	Helen Jacobs - S. Palfrey	C. Babcock - D. Andrus	4-6, 6-3, 6-4
1935	H. Jacobs - S. Palfrey Fabyan	C. Babcock - D. Andrus	6-4, 6-2
1936	M. Van Ryn - C. Babcock	Helen Jacobs - S. Palfrey Fabyan	9-7, 2-6, 6-4
1937	S. Palfrey Fabyan - A. Marble	M. Van Ryn - C. Babcock	7-5, 6-4
1938	S. Palfrey Fabyan - A. Marble	R. Mathieu - J. Jedrzejowska	6-8, 6-4, 6-3
1939	S. Palfrey Fabyan - A. Marble	Kay Stammers - F. James Hammersley	7-5, 8-6
1940	S. Palfrey Fabyan - A. Marble	Dorothy Bundy - M. Van Ryn	6-4, 6-3
1941	S. P. Fabyan - M. Osborne	Dorothy Bundy - Pauline Betz	3-6, 6-1, 6-4
1942	Louise Brough - M. Osborne	Pauline Betz - Doris Hart	2-6, 7-5, 6-0
1943	Louise Brough - M. Osborne	Patricia C. Todd - Mary A. Prentiss	6-1, 6-3
1944	Louise Brough - M. Osborne	Pauline Betz - Doris Hart	4-6, 6-4, 6-3
1945	Louise Brough - M. Osborne	Pauline Betz - Doris Hart	6-3, 6-3
1946	Louise Brough - M. Osborne	Patricia C. Todd - Mary A. Prentiss	6-1, 6-3
1947	Louise Brough - M. Osborne	Patricia C. Todd - Doris Hart	5-7, 6-3, 7-5
1948	Louise Brough - M. O. duPont	Patricia C. Todd - Doris Hart	6-4, 8-10, 6-1
1949	Louise Brough - M. O. duPont	Doris Hart - Shirley Fry	6-4, 10-8
1950	Louise Brough - M. O. duPont	Doris Hart - Shirley Fry	6-2, 6-3
1951	Shirley Fry - Doris Hart	Nancy Chaffee - Patricia C. Todd	6-4, 6-2
1952	Shirley Fry - Doris Hart	Louise Brough - Maureen Connolly	10-8, 6-4
1953	Shirley Fry - Doris Hart	Louise Brough - M. O. duPont	6-2, 7-9, 9-7
1954	Shirley Fry - Doris Hart	Louise Brough - M. O. duPont	6-4, 6-4
1955	Louise Brough - M. O. duPont	Doris Hart - Shirley Fry	6-3, 1-6, 6-3
1956	Louise Brough - M. O. duPont	Betty R. Pratt - Shirley Fry	6-3, 6-0
1957	Louise Brough - M. O. duPont	Althea Gibson - Darlene Hard	6-2, 7-5
1958	Jeanne Arth - Darlene Hard	Althea Gibson - Maria Bueno	2-6, 6-3, 6-4
1959	Jeanne Arth - Darlene Hard	Maria Bueno - Sally Moore	6-2, 6-3
1960	Maria Bueno - Darlene Hard	Ann Haydon - Deidre Catt	6-1, 6-1
1961	Darlene Hard - Lesley Turner	Edda Buding - Yola Ramirez	6-4, 5-7, 6-0
1962	Darlene Hard - Maria Bueno	K. H. Susman - Billie Jean Moffitt	4-6, 6-3, 6-2
1963	R. Ebbern - Margaret Smith	Darlene Hard - Maria Bueno	4-6, 10-8, 6-3
1964	B. J. Moffitt - K. H. Susman	Margaret Smith - Lesley Turner	3-6, 6-2, 6-4
1965	C. C. Graebner - N. Richey	B. J. Moffitt - K. H. Susman	6-4, 6-4
1966	Maria Bueno - N. Richey	B. J. Moffitt King - Rosie Casals	6-3, 6-4
1967	Rosie Casals - B. J. King	Mary Ann Eisel - Donna F. Fales	4-6, 6-3, 6-4

U.S. OPEN

Year	Champions	Runners-up	Score
1968	M. Bueno - M. Smith Court	B. J. King - Rosie Casals	4-6, 9-7, 8-6
1969	Francoise Durr - Darlene Hard	M. Smith Court - Virginia Wade	0-6, 6-4, 6-4
1970	M. Smith Court - J. T. Dalton	Rosie Casals - Virginia Wade	6-3, 6-4
1971	Rosie Casals - J. T. Dalton	G. S. Chanfreau - Francoise Durr	6-3, 6-3
1972	Francoise Durr - Betty Stove	M. Smith Court - Virginia Wade	6-3, 1-6, 6-3
1973	M. Smith Court - V. Wade	B. J. King - Rosie Casals	3-6, 6-3, 7-5
1974	Rosie Casals - B. J. King	Francoise Durr - Betty Stove	7-6, 6-7, 6-4
1975	M. Smith Court - V. Wade	B. J. King - Rosie Casals	7-5, 2-6, 7-5
1976	Delina Boshoff - Ilana Kloss	Olga Morozova - Virginia Wade	6-1, 6-4
1977	M. Navratilova - B. Stove	Renee Richards - B. G. Stuart	6-1, 7-6
1978	B. J. King - M. Navratilova	K. M. Reid - Wendy Turnbull	7-6, 6-4
1979	Betty Stove - Wendy Turnbull	B. J. King - Martina Navratilova	7-5, 6-3
1980	B. J. King - M. Navratilova	Pam Shriver - Betty Stove	7-6, 7-5
1981	Anne Smith - Kathy Jordan	Rosie Casals - Wendy Turnbull	6-3, 6-3
1982	Rosie Casals - Wendy Turnbull	Sharon Walsh - Barbara Potter	6-4, 6-4
1983	Pam Shriver - M. Navratilova	Rosalyn Fairbank - Candy Reynolds	6-7, 6-1, 6-3

Year	Champions	Runners-up	Score
1984	Pam Shriver - M. Navratilova	Anne Hobbs - Wendy Turnbull	6-2, 6-4
1985	C. Kohde-Kilsch - H. Sukova	Martina Navratilova - Pam Shriver	6-7, 6-2, 6-3
1986	Pam Shriver - M. Navratilova	Hana Mandlikova - Wendy Turnbull	6-4, 3-6, 6-3
1987	Pam Shriver - M. Navratilova	Kathy Jordan - E. Sayers Smylie	5-7, 6-4, 6-2
1988	Gigi Fernandez - R. White	Patty Fendick - Jill Hetherington	6-4, 6-1
1989	H. Mandlikova - M. Navratilova	Mary Joe Fernandez - Pam Shriver	5-7, 6-4, 6-4
1990	Gigi Fernandez - M. Navratilova	Jana Novotna - Helena Sukova	6-2, 6-4
1991	Pam Shriver - Natasha Zvereva	Jana Novotna - Larisa Neiland	6-4, 4-6, 7-6
1992	Gigi Fernandez - N. Zvereva	Jana Novotna - Larisa Neiland	7-6, 6-1
1993	A. Sánchez Vicario - H. Sukova	Amanda Coetzer - Ines Gorrochategui	6-4, 6-2
1994	J. Novotna - A. Sánchez Vicario	Katerina Maleeva - Robin White	6-3, 6-3
1995	Gigi Fernandez - N. Zvereva	Brenda Schultz-McCarthy - R. Stubbs	7-5, 6-3
1996	Gigi Fernandez - N. Zvereva	Jana Novotna - A. Sánchez Vicario	1-6, 6-1, 6-4

National Mixed Doubles Finals

Year	Champions	Runners-up	Score
1892	M. Cahill - C. Hobart	E. Moore - R. Beach	6-1, 6-3
1893	E. Roosevelt - C. Hobart	E. Bankson - R. Willson, Jr.	6-1, 4-6, 10-8, 6-1
1894	J. Atkinson - E. Fischer	Mrs. McFadden - G. Remack, Jr.	6-3, 6-2, 6-1
1895	J. Atkinson - E. Fischer	A. Williams - M. Fielding	4-6, 8-6, 6-2
1896	J. Atkinson - E. Fischer	A. Williams - M. Fielding	6-2, 6-3, 6-3
1897	L. Henson - D. L. Magruder	M. Banks - R. A. Griffin	6-4, 6-3, 7-5
1898	C. Neely - E. Fischer	H. Chapman - J. A. Hill	6-2, 6-4, 8-6
1899	E. Rastall - A. Hoskins	J. Craven - J. Gardner	6-4, 6-0, default
1900	M. Hunnewell - A. Codman	T. Shaw - G. Atkinson	11-9, 6-3, 6-1
1901	M. Jones - R. Little	M. McAteer - C. Stevens	6-4, 6-4, 7-5
1902	E. Moore - W. Grant	E. Rastall - A. Hoskins	6-2, 6-1
1903	H. Chapman - H. Allen	C. Neely - W. H. Rowland	6-4, 7-5
1904	E. Moore - W. Grant	M. Sutton - T. Dallas	6-2, 6-1
1905	A. Schultz Hobart - C. Hobart	E. Moore - E. Dewhurst	6-2, 6-4
1906	S. Coffin - E. Dewhurst	M. Johnson - W. Johnson	6-3, 7-5
1907	M. Sayers - W. Johnson	N. Wildey - W. M. Tilden	6-1, 7-5
1908	E. Rotch - N. Niles	L. Hammond - R. Little	6-4, 4-6, 6-4
1909	H. Hotchkiss - W. Johnson	L. Hammond - R. Little	6-2, 6-0
1910	H. Hotchkiss - J. Carpenter, Jr.	E. Wildey - H. M. Tilden	6-2, 6-2
1911	H. Hotchkiss - W. Johnson	E. Wildey - H. M. Tilden	6-4, 6-4
1912	M. K. Browne - R. Williams	El. Sears - W. Clothier	6-4, 2-6, 11-9
1913	M. K. Browne - W. Tilden	D. Green - C. S. Rogers	7-5, 7-5
1914	M. K. Browne - W. Tilden	M. Myers - J. R. Rowland	6-1, 6-4
1915	H. H. Wightman - H. Johnson	M. Bjurstedt - I. Wright	6-0, 6-1
1916	El. Sears - W. Davis	F. Ballin - W. Tilden	6-4, 7-5
1917	M. Bjurstedt - I. Wright	F. Ballin - W. Tilden	10-12, 6-1, 6-3
1918	H. H. Wightman - I. Wright	M. Bjurstedt - F. Alexander	6-2, 6-4
1919	M. Zinderstein - V. Richards	F. Ballin - W. Tilden	2-6, 11-9, 6-2
1920	H. H. Wightman - W. Johnson	M. B. Mallory - C. Biddle	6-4, 6-3
1921	M. K. Browne - W. Johnston	M. B. Mallory - W. Tilden	3-6, 6-4, 6-3
1922	M. B. Mallory - W. Tilden	H. Wills - H. Kinsey	6-4, 6-3
1923	M. B. Mallory - W. Tilden	K. McKane - J. Hawkes	6-3, 2-6, 10-8
1924	H. Wills - V. Richards	M. B. Mallory - W. Tilden	6-8, 7-5, 6-0
1925	K. McKane - J. Hawkes	E. Harvey - V. Richards	6-2, 6-4
1926	E. Ryan - J. Borotra	H. H. Wightman - R. Lacoste	6-4, 7-5
1927	E. Bennett - H. Cochet	H. H. Wightman - R. Lacoste	6-2, 0-6, 6-3
1928	H. Wills - J. Hawkes	E. Cross - G. Moon	6-1, 6-3
1929	B. Nuthall - G. Lott, Jr.	P. Covell - H. Austin	6-3, 6-3
1930	E. Cross - W. Allison	M. Morrill - F. Shields	6-4, 6-4
1931	B. Nuthall - G. Lott, Jr.	A. McCune Harper - W. Allison	6-3, 6-3
1932	S. Palfrey - F. Perry	H. Jacobs - E. Vines	6-3, 7-5
1933	E. Ryan - E. Vines	S. Palfrey - G. Lott, Jr.	11-9, 6-1
1934	H. Jacobs - G. Lott, Jr.	E. Ryan - L. Stoefen	4-6, 13-11, 6-2
1935	S. Palfrey Fabyan - E. Maier	K. Stammers - R. Menzel	6-4, 4-6, 6-3
1936	A. Marble - G. Mako	S. Palfrey Fabyan - D. Budge	6-3, 6-2
1937	S. Palfrey Fabyan - D. Budge	S. Henrotin - Y. Petra	6-2, 8-10, 6-0
1938	A. Marble - D. Budge	T. Coyne - J. Bromwich	6-1, 6-2
1939	A. Marble - H. Hopman	S. Palfrey Fabyan - E. Cooke	9-7, 6-1
1940	A. Marble - R. Riggs	D. Bundy - J. Kramer	9-7, 6-1
1941	S. Palfrey Cooke - J. Kramer	P. Betz - R. Riggs	4-6, 6-4, 6-4
1942	A. L. Brough - F. Schroeder	P. Canning Todd - A. Russell	3-6, 6-1, 6-4
1943	M. Osborne - W. Talbert	P. Betz - F. Segura	10-8, 6-4
1944	M. Osborne - W. Talbert	D. Bundy - D. McNeill	6-2, 6-4
1945	M. Osborne - W. Talbert	D. Hart - R. Falkenberg	6-4, 6-4
1946	M. Osborne - W. Talbert	A. L. Brough - R. Kimbrell	6-3, 6-4
1947	A. L. Brough - J. Bromwich	G. Moran - F. Segura	6-3, 6-1
1948	A. L. Brough - T. Brown	M. O. duPont - W. Talbert	6-4, 6-4
1949	A. L. Brough - E. Sturgess	M. O. duPont - W. Talbert	4-6, 6-3, 7-5
1950	M. O. duPont - K. McGregor	D. Hart - F. Sedgman	6-4, 3-6, 6-3
1951	D. Hart - F. Sedgman	S. Fry - M. Rose	6-3, 6-2
1952	D. Hart - F. Sedgman	T. C. Long - L. Hoad	6-3, 7-5
1953	D. Hart - E. V. Seixas	J. Sampson - R. Hartwig	6-2, 4-6, 6-4
1954	D. Hart - E. V. Seixas	M. O. duPont - K. Rosewall	4-6, 6-1, 6-1

Year	Champions	Runners-up	Score
1955	D. Hart - E. V. Seixas	S. Fry - L. Hoad	9-7, 6-1
1956	M. O. duPont - K. Rosewall	D. Hard - L. Hoad	9-7, 6-1
1957	A. Gibson - K. Neilsen	D. Hard - R. Howe	6-3, 9-7
1958	M. O. duPont - N. Fraser	M. Bueno - A. Olmedo	6-3, 3-6, 9-7
1959	M. O. duPont - N. Fraser	J. Hopps - R. Mark	7-5, 13-15, 6-2
1960	M. O. duPont - N. Fraser	M.Bueno - A. Palafox	6-3, 6-2
1961	M. Smith - R. Mark	D. Hard - D. Ralston	default
1962	M. Smith - F. Stolle	L. Turner - F. Froehling, III	7-5, 6-2
1963	M. Smith - K. Fletcher	J. Tegart - E. Rubinoff	3-6, 8-6, 6-2
1964	M. Smith - J. Newcombe	J. Tegart - E. Rubinoff	10-8, 4-6, 6-3
1965	M. Smith - F. Stolle	J. Tegart - F. Froehling, III	6-2, 6-2
1966	D. F. Fales - O. Davidson	C. H. Aucamp - E. Rubinoff	6-1, 6-3
1967	B. J. King - O. Davidson	R. Casals - S. Smith	6-3, 6-2

U.S. Open

Year	Champions	Runners-up	Score
1968	not held		
1969	M. Smith Court - M. Riessen	F. Durr - D. Ralston	7-5, 6-3
1970	M. Smith Court - M. Riessen	J. Tegart Dalton - F. McMillan	6-4, 6-4
1971	B. J. King - O. Davidson	B. Stove - R. Maud	6-3, 7-5
1972	M. Smith Court - M. Riessen	R. Casals - I. Nastase	6-3, 7-5
1973	B. J. King - O. Davidson	M. Smith Court - M. Riessen	6-3, 3-6, 7-6
1974	P. Teeguarden - G. Masters	C. Evert - J. Connors	6-1, 7-6
1975	R. Casals - R. Stockton	B. J. King - F. Stolle	6-3, 7-6
1976	B. J. King - P. Dent	B. Stove - F. McMillan	3-6, 6-2, 7-5
1977	B. Stove - F. McMillan	B. J. King - V. Gerulaitis	6-2, 3-6, 6-3
1978	B. Stove - F. McMillan	B. J. King - R. Ruffels	6-3, 7-6
1979	G. Stevens - R. Hewitt	B. Stove - F. McMillan	6-3, 7-5
1980	W. Turnbull - M. Riessen	B. Stove - F. McMillan	7-5, 6-2
1981	A. Smith - K. Curren	J. Russell - S. Denton	6-4, 7-6
1982	A. Smith - K. Curren	B. Potter - F. Taygan	6-7, 7-6, 7-6
1983	E. Sayers - J. Fitzgerald	B. Potter - F. Taygan	3-6, 6-3, 6-4
1984	Man. Maleeva - Tom Gullikson	E. Sayers - J. Fitzgerald	2-6, 7-5, 6-4
1985	M. Navratilova - H. Gunthardt	E. Sayers Smylie - J. Fitzgerald	6-3, 6-4
1986	R. Reggi - S. Casal	M. Navratilova - P. Fleming	6-4, 6-4
1987	M. Navratilova - E. Sánchez	B. Nagelsen - P. Annacone	6-4, 6-7, 7-6
1988	J. Novotna - J. Pugh	E. Sayers Smylie - P. McEnroe	7-5, 6-3
1989	R. White - S. Cannon	M. McGrath - R. Leach	3-6, 6-2, 7-5
1990	E. Sayers Smylie - T. Woodbridge	N. Zvereva - J. Pugh	6-4, 6-2
1991	M. Bollegraf - T. Nijssen	A. Sánchez Vicario - E. Sánchez	6-2, 7-6
1992	N. Provis - M. Woodforde	H. Sukova - T. Nijssen	4-6, 6-3, 6-3
1993	H. Sukova - T. Woodbridge	M. Navratilova - M. Woodforde	6-3, 7-6
1994	E. Reinach - P. Galbraith	J. Novotna - T. Woodbridge	6-2, 6-4
1995	M. McGrath - M. Lucena	G. Fernandez - C. Suk	6-4, 6-4
1996	L.Raymond - P. Galbraith	M. Bollegraf - R. Leach	7-6, 7-6

Venues

Although the five major championships — men's and women's singles, men's and women's doubles, and mixed doubles — have been played together as a part of the U.S. Open program in recent years, such was not the case during much of the history of these championships. Here are the sites for the championships in all events since 1881:

Men's Singles

1881-1914	The Casino, Newport, R.I.
1915-20	West Side Tennis Club, N.Y.
1921-23	Germantown Cricket Club, Philadelphia
1924-77	West Side Tennis Club
1978-	USTA National Tennis Center

Men's Doubles

1881-86	The Casino, Newport
1987	Orange Tennis Club, Mountain Station, N.J.
1888-89	Staten Island Cricket Club, N.Y.
1890-92	The Casino, Newport
1893	St. George Cricket Club, Chicago
1894-1914	The Casino, Newport
1915-16	West Side Tennis Club
1917-33	Longwood Cricket Club, Boston
1934	Germantown Cricket Club
1935-41	Longwood Cricket Club
1942-45	West Side Tennis Club
1946-67	Longwood Cricket Club
1968-77	West Side Tennis Club
1978-	USTA National Tennis Center

Women's Singles

1887-1920	Philadelphia Cricket Club
1921-1977	West Side Tennis Club
1978-	USTA National Tennis Center

Women's Doubles

1887-1920	Philadelphia Cricket Club
1921-33	West Side Tennis Club
1934	Germantown Cricket Club
1935-41	Longwood Cricket Club
1942-45	West Side Cricket Club
1946-67	Longwood Cricket Club
1968-77	West Side Tennis Club
1978-	USTA National Tennis Center

Mixed Doubles

1892-1920	Philadelphia Cricket Club
1921-34	West Side Tennis Club
1935-41	Longwood Cricket Club
1942-67	West Side Tennis Club
1969-77	West Side Tennis Club
1978-	USTA National Tennis Center

PHOTOGRAPHY CREDITS

INDEX